Teaching Machines

tech.edu
A Hopkins Series on Education and Technology

Teaching Machines

Learning from the Intersection of

Education and Technology

Bill Ferster

JOHNS HOPKINS UNIVERSITY PRESS   BALTIMORE

© 2014 Johns Hopkins University Press
All rights reserved. Published 2014
Printed in the United States of America on acid-free paper
9 8 7 6 5 4 3 2 1

Johns Hopkins University Press
2715 North Charles Street
Baltimore, Maryland 21218-4363
www.press.jhu.edu

Library of Congress Cataloging-in-Publication Data

Ferster, Bill, 1956–
    Teaching machines / Bill Ferster.
        pages cm. — (Tech.edu: A Hopkins Series on Education and Technology)
    Includes bibliographical references and index.
    ISBN 978-1-4214-1540-6 (hardcover : alk. paper) — ISBN 978-1-4214-1541-3
(electronic) — ISBN 1-4214-1540-2 (hardcover : alk. paper) — ISBN 1-4214-1541-0
(electronic)   1. Educational technology.   I. Title.
    LB1028.3.F49 2014
    371.33—dc23   2014004982

A catalog record for this book is available from the British Library.

Special discounts are available for bulk purchases of this book. For more information,
please contact Special Sales at 410-516-6936 or specialsales@press.jhu.edu.

Johns Hopkins University Press uses environmentally friendly book materials,
including recycled text paper that is composed of at least 30 percent post-consumer
waste, whenever possible.

For Marilyn B. Gilbert and Charles B. Ferster

Contents

Preface

With the recent media focus on MOOCs,* the Khan Academy, and online learning, it's easy to forget that people have been looking how technology can facilitate teaching for a very long time. From the early days of educational film, through B. F. Skinner's programmed instruction, and into the myriad of e-learning initiatives, educators have been trying to automate instruction.

Albert Einstein once defined insanity as "doing the same thing over and over again and expecting different results." This book is a critical look at past initiatives in automating instruction, so we can understand them from historic, technological, theoretical, economic, and political perspectives and hopefully learn from their successes and failures.

In this book, I examine efforts to automate instruction, provide some overarching commentary, offer insight into current and future uses of instructional technology, and portray people trying to make a difference in education. I tell these stories through the eyes of those who developed and promoted the innovations because many of the same issues and presumptions exist in today's automated instructional tools. The book depicts the people who believed that technology can contribute to learning; in the process, it exposes their thought processes and the hurdles they worked to overcome.

In recounting this history, I will be as objective as is possible but will also provide my personal perspective as a designer, educator, and technologist. I have an odd combination of pessimism about previous efforts to automate learning coupled with respect for the innovators and what technology can bring to society when thoughtfully introduced, and I try to impart both perspectives.

---

*MOOCs, or massive open online courses, are offered online to huge numbers of participants. Providers of these courses include Udacity, edX (developed by Harvard University and the Massachusetts Institute of Technology), and Coursera.

Figure P.1. The author in a "Skinner box" made by Ben Wykoff, an early teaching machine pioneer, 1956.
Author's collection

My own childhood offers a unique perspective on learning machines. My experimental-psychologist father was a colleague of the behaviorist B. F. Skinner at Harvard University in the 1950s, and I grew up enmeshed in the small, hubris-filled world that was 1960s behaviorism. Like all dutiful children of that world, I spent my earliest months in a "Skinner box," which, unlike the boxes Skinner used for pigeons, merely provided a comfortable environment for me to roll around in and, of course, bragging rights among my parents' peers (figure P.1).

My siblings and I sometimes worked in my father's lab after school, earning a nickel for each programmed instruction card we made for the teaching machines he used in his research projects. Teaching and learning were common dinner topics, as was gossip about the leading behavioral researchers of the day, many of whom are portrayed in this book. In middle school, I learned geometry using a teaching machine (which took only half the time to master rather than taking the class in the traditional manner).

The behaviorists of that time believed they had cracked the secret of how people learn, by extending their ground-breaking work on animal learning in carefully controlled experiments. We have since found that human learning is a more complicated process than they initially conceived, but their influence, both positive and negative, has cast a long shadow on education in general, and on educational technology in particular.

How This Book Is Organized

The kinds of teaching machines explored in the chapters that follow are particular innovations framed in unique environments, but several common threads emerge from these individual stories to provide useful connections to a larger narrative. The gist of that narrative is that there has been a long history of people trying to use technology to facilitate education and that those efforts have consistently failed to live up to the promises of their promoters.

To parse out the reasons for these failures, I use the following lenses to explore each effort's history, influences, contexts, and impact in a narrative form, with the lives of the machine's innovators as the foundation:

- *Personal.* The lives and personal influences of the innovators themselves provide rich threads to weave with other factors and offer a fuller and more interesting story. As it turns out, the innovators were complicated, quirky, and fascinating people whose relationships and influences often interconnected.
- *Historical.* The historical context in which the machines were invented had a strong influence on why and how they were created, flourished, and ultimately failed.
- *Theoretical.* The theoretical consensus on how people teach and learn is constantly evolving, and teaching machines were often used as "Trojan horses" for various movements (particularly behaviorism), which had strong influences on their design, efficacy, and adoption.
- *Economic and business.* Machines of all kinds are employed because of a strong economic motivation to reduce costs through automation, and teaching machines are no exception. Many of the proponents of

teaching machines actively pursued commercial interests surrounding their academic efforts.

- *Political.* Few fields are as political as education, particularly in K–12. Teaching machines have been seen as both the great equalizer and the great divider along racial, socioeconomic/equity, and academic-ability lines. Some have viewed them as a means to disintermediate the role of teachers and even entire academic institutions.
- *Technological.* The development of new technologies provides a constant source of new possibilities to be exploited. Reinforced by the arrogance that "this changes everything," advocates argue that new technologies will solve the problem better than previous efforts.

Each chapter looks at a specific genre of teaching machine, from mass instruction through the postal service to Internet-based tools. I do not explore every effort to develop learning technologies but focus instead on those that try to disintermediate the role of the school or teacher and to combine content knowledge with pedagogy.

The narrative is not strictly chronological, as the different genres are influenced by different preceding events and lines of thought. In some cases I take time to examine these precursors and their effect on the primary subject's development. Each chapter concludes with an assessment of the genre's impact on education, its successes and failures, and its influence on future developments.

"Sage on the Stage" looks at technologies that replicate traditional learning experiences, such as the classroom lecture and books. The first real attempt to provide learning at a distance occurred in the late nineteenth century, with correspondence courses that sent printed material via the postal system. In the 1910s, schools began to purchase motion picture projectors for the classroom. By the turn of the twenty-first century, the Massachusetts Institute of Technology and other elite universities were posting videos of classroom lectures online for anyone to access for free. Salman Khan took full advantage of the newly available capabilities of YouTube by posting videos he created using screencasting* tools to create videos of him teaching mathematics lessons over a "virtual chalkboard."

---

*A *screencast* is a movie that digitally captures the screen of someone using a computer, often with a soundtrack of the person narrating what he or she is doing.

"Step by Step" explores the world of programmed instruction, primarily through the eyes of psychologists Sidney Pressey and B. F. Skinner, to see how their objectivist/behaviorist perspectives shaped their views on machines that teach. The fear provoked by the Soviet Union's 1957 surprise launching of the Sputnik satellite, coupled with a shortage of qualified teachers, encouraged psychologists in the United States to create 1960s versions of today's Silicon Valley startups, where companies were formed and to address perceived deficits in the educational system. Silicon Valley computer scientists in the late twentieth century inherited this model, making their own forays into the world of educational business.

"Byte by Byte" investigates what happened when computer scientists took the reins of teaching machines from the psychologists. Their solutions relied more on the emerging digital computer and networking developments than on particular ideological learning constructs. The introduction of smaller and faster computers prompted some developers to look beyond simply presenting information and assessing its absorption. The new technology offered an opportunity for a richer set of interactions with the learner, an environment closer to a tutorial. Artificial intelligence (AI) researchers looked for ways to apply the newly emerging AI techniques to teaching.

"From the Cloud" examines the role of the Internet in education. The Web has been touted as a powerful environment for teaching. Up to now, we have seen only "filmed plays"* in Marshall McLuhan's sense, which merely take advantage of the frictionless delivery of content. Truly interactive applications that couple the networked nature of the Internet with the power of modern personal computers have a great, but as yet unrealized, potential. I explore the role of learning management systems (LMS), immersive experiences such as simulations and Second Life, the popular Khan Academy videos, e-learning, and, of course, MOOCs to automate education to levels well beyond the capabilities of earlier technologies.

"Making Sense of Teaching Machines" draws from previous chapters to flesh out some common themes and to comment on issues that must be addressed in designing future teaching machines. Several technological

*Marshall McLuhan observed that new types of media initially replicate the existing forms, at least until they establish themselves as a medium that exploits their unique features. The first movies were little more than films of dramatic stage plays.

trends are likely to influence how tomorrow's machines will work: learners from every economic status and geographic region are getting better access and faster Internet service; more and more high-quality educational resources are available online; there are better techniques for finding and making sense of those resources; and finally, improved natural language and semantic processing techniques are making machines more conversational and capable of making better sense of a learner's written or spoken responses.

Today, a majority of learners carries small, personally addressable, Internet-connected computer workstations in the palms of their hands, a development that would have amazed the engineers who made the older teaching machines. These devices have the potential to offer endless possibilities to those who design the next generation of educational technology.

It should be clear by this point that we have much to learn from the long history of trying to automate instruction. The good ideas, political missteps, technological progress, and ideological hubris all provide much-needed context for our current and future teaching machines.

I wish to thank the following people for their help in the research and production for this project: Ludy Benjamin, Don Bitzer, Greg Britton, Peter Brusilovsky, John Bunch, Allen Calvin, Dave Cormier, Jan Everote, Elizabeth Fanning, Yitna Firdyiwek, Susan Ferster, Roger Geyer, Marilyn Gilbert, Beth Harris, Dov Jacobson, Joe Kett, Tom Panelas, Chuck Rieger, Ben Sawyer, Michael Zuckerman, and the amazing staff of the Alderman Library at the University of Virginia. Reports on the death of libraries have been *greatly* exaggerated.

Teaching Machines

1

Introduction

The allure of educational technology is easy to understand. In almost every other area of our modern world, machines have significantly contributed to modern life, but they are largely missing from our schools. A nineteenth-century visitor would feel quite at home in a modern classroom, even at our most elite institutions of higher learning. Even online education, which is by definition technology-based, tends to use new technology to mimic the actions of older practices, simply using the Internet to deliver page-based content, quizzes, and other assessments or digitized versions of classroom lectures rather than delivering the material on paper or in person.

People have looked to machines to solve issues in most other endeavors in their lives, hoping to gain improved efficiency, cost, and time savings. So it is not surprising that technology has been employed for both noble (better learning outcomes) and less than noble reasons (teacher proofing).*

What Is Educational Technology?

Teachers have employed tools to assist them in educating others for hundreds of years, using their era's state-of-the-art technology. They have started simply, from slate boards used to facilitate the mastery of penmanship and spelling to immersive and exploratory virtual environments that are often guided by an elaborate base of theoretical literature that helps build critical-thinking skills.

Teacher proofing is the name given to the practice of limiting the autonomy of individual teachers to produce a more uniform and controlled experience. Various techniques include strict curricular content control and rigid pacing guidelines, high-stakes testing, standardized textbooks, and practices such as direct instruction.

What people mean when they talk about educational or instructional technology has changed over the past hundred years. Sometimes they are responding to the state of the technology itself; at other times, the meaning depends on whether theoretical or pedagogical issues need be considered along with the physical devices. Robert Heinich and his colleagues adapted the economist John Kenneth Galbraith's overall definition of technology to education: "the approach of applying our scientific knowledge about human learning to the practical task of teaching and learning."[1] This definition implies a broader role for educational technology than simply more and better physical devices. The solution may indeed require gizmos and gadgets, but Heinich's work suggests a more holistic approach, one that intimates some method behind the madness that provides some rationale for what particular technological approach might be most effective.

One of the earliest innovations that directly married pedagogy and content knowledge into a physical device was the hornbook, introduced in 1467. The hornbook was "a leaf of written or printed paper, pasted to a board, and covered with horn, for children to learn their letters, and to prevent their being torn or daubed."[2] The Pilgrims brought the first hornbooks to America, and they continued to be imported from England until the Revolutionary War disrupted trade (figure 1.1).

In the 1700s, educational tools tended to be centered on the student rather than the teacher, such as goose-quill pens, ink, and paper. Student's families provided the pens, and since the pens required a very time-consuming process of cutting and mending during class time, teachers were often hired for their quill-fixing prowess rather than their teaching ability. The ink, boiled down from the bark of swamp maple trees, was often weak, translucent, and troublesome to read. Paper was expensive and scarce, so poorer schools relied on unruled birch bark cut into 13-by-17-inch sheets (known as foolscap size). The students would fold the larger sheet into more manageable sections, leaving the rough bark side as the cover.[3]

In the nineteenth century, the focus of instructional tools shifted from the student to the teacher. In 1813, a Boston school reformer noted, "I attended a mathematical school and . . . saw what now I trust is indispensible in every school—the blackboard."[4] These rudimentary whole-class presentation drawing devices presaged their more technologically sophisticated progeny, the digital projector and "smart board," now commonplace in most K–12 and college classrooms.

Figure 1.1. Examples of early horn-books.
From Andrew Tuer, *History of the Horn-Book* (New York: Charles Scribner's Sons, 1896)

Between 1920 and 1980, educational technology was almost synonymous with the term *audiovisual technology*, characterized as taking a media-based approach to present prepared curricular materials to the whole class using a variety of technological devices, beginning with magic lantern slide projectors (figure 1.2); film, filmstrip, and slide projectors; and finally, television sets showing live broadcasts or playing videotape. The locus of attention moved from the teacher to an external information source channeled by technology.[5]

The Textbook

It is impossible to talk about educational technology without recognizing the primacy of the book as the principal delivery mechanism of human thought up through the present day. The basic form of the textbook began in the eighteenth century as a question-and-answer sequence designed to mimic the form of a religious catechism.[6] This style of organization remained popular in the nineteenth century because of a lack of trained teachers.[7] In a sense, this was a very early example of "teacher proofing."

Figure 1.2. The magic lantern projector, an early classroom audiovisual tool.
Courtesy of Andrei Niemimäki

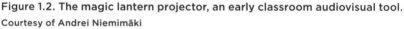

Some of the first books used in instruction in the United States were Noah Webster's popular 1783 blue-backed spellers, which provided a structured and age-progressed method to present words and offered rules for pronunciation and strategies for learners, such as breaking up longer words into their constituent parts. The speller proved so popular that Webster subsequently added a grammar and reader to his offerings, which spawned 385 editions in his lifetime, with more than 60 million copies sold by 1890.[8]

In 1837, William Holmes McGuffey began to write a series of readers, which would become some of the most popular textbooks of the period, selling over twice as many copies as Webster's "blue-backed" speller, and, interestingly enough, continues to be used by parents home-schooling their children.[9] McGuffey was a licensed Presbyterian preacher who delivered over 3,000 sermons during his brief career, taught philosophy at Miami University in Oxford, Ohio, and worked unsuccessfully as school administrator. Publisher Winthrop Smith approached him in 1836 to write a series of readers to be used in schools. The readers (figure 1.3) initially contained a large amount of religious instruction that took the form of a "religious meditation," but later editions replaced the emphasis on religion with moralism.[10]

McGuffey was apparently not a particularly astute businessman when Smith offered him a deal that provided a 10 percent royalty on the proceeds, but only up to $1,000 in total royalties, with the publisher holding the copyright thereafter. Historian Charles Carpenter remarked, "Had McGuffey made contracts as did [Noah] Webster, he probably would have become one of the wealthy men of the country." Apparently McGuffey's moralism only went so far: the publisher of a competing reader, the Worcester Readers, sued Smith for plagiarism in 1838, serving his company with a federal restraining order until McGuffey removed the pilfered passages and eventually paid the competitor $2,000 in damages.[11]

Eventually, schools replaced the readers with age-progressed textbooks that had less emphasis on myths and fables and increasingly included stories about idealized white middle-class families, like Dick and Jane, where the moralism of McGuffey's time was more implicit than explicit. "In the 1920s, the textbook stood alone," textbook publisher Grant Benton reminisced; in the 1950s, "there were more provisions for individual differences, graded exercises, and keyed bibliographies."[12]

As public education expanded across America in the mid-nineteenth century, providing taxpayer-funded primary education, normal schools (public and private colleges for training new teachers) began to spring up. These schools often used a pedagogical approach known as object teaching, advocated by the Swiss educator Johann Pestalozzi. This approach laid the groundwork for the progressive education movement many years later by encouraging a more child-centered and exploratory approach to learning than the rote memorization used up to that point.

Object teaching's aim was to provide a direct link to an understanding of the item being learned, not just its name. Basal classes, such as arithmetic and spelling, were considered a means to an end, not the primary reason

Figure 1.3. Cover of McGuffey's *Fifth Eclectic Reader* (1921).
Courtesy of Daniel Dyer

for instruction. The ability to understand and use numbers, not just rote skills involved in long division, was the chief objective of mathematics lessons. The teacher guided the students to explore and ultimately internalize these intuitive understandings and use them as tools to understanding the world.[13] Eerily prescient of educational technology's invasion of the classroom, Pestalozzi wrote at the turn of the nineteenth century, "I wish to wrest education from the outworn order of doddering old teaching hacks as well as from the new-fangled order of cheap, artificial teaching tricks, and entrust it to the eternal powers of nature herself."[14] As normal schools graduated more and more teachers, and ultimately textbook authors, Pestalozzi's object teaching philosophy began to change the nature of textbooks used in American schools.

Books have always had a strong embedded political component to them, especially in the ways their authors and editors decide what to communicate and how to frame that content. Textbooks are no exception, and the public nature of funding often creates debate. A good example of this occurred in 1995, with the controversy surrounding the National Standards for History. These standards sought to provide a suggested curriculum for the study of American history that would guide teachers, textbook authors, and test-makers. This guidance is all the more copious now in the age of high-stakes testing, where teachers tend to "teach to the test."

In 1989, the National Endowment for the Humanities (NEH), led by Lynne Cheney,* and the Department of Education tried to codify what the expectations should be for the instruction of history. In its zeal to be all-inclusive, the specific recommendations as to what events should be covered in the curriculum and why, drew a groundswell of opposition from ideologues at both ends of the political spectrum, with opponents criticizing it as being radically multicultural and overly politically correct.

Just prior to the standards' publication, in 1995, a "right-wing assault"[15] was launched by none other than the original funder of the standards, Lynne Cheney. She engaged right-wing allies in the press and punditry to make claims that the Clinton administration had subverted the standards' original mission. Even though there had initially been strong bipartisan support for the effort, public outcry was so fierce that Senator Slade Gorton (R-WA) sponsored a nonbinding resolution to reject the standards, claiming they were "ideology masquerading as history."[16] The Senate voted on the resolution, which passed by a resounding 99 to 1, with Senator Bennett Johnston (D-LA) abstaining, on the grounds he had actually read the standards and wanted "something with teeth in it."[17] It was not altogether clear whether any of the other senators had even looked at the document

---

*Lynne Cheney is the wife of Dick Cheney, secretary of defense (1989–1993) and vice president (2001–2009).

or were simply reacting to the political rhetoric thick in the air. What is clear is that textbooks and the content they cover have strong ideological and political components.

Educational Technology in Schools

So why is technology so conspicuously absent from education? Or if it is used at all, why is its role minor and supportive, or, as in the case of online instruction, why is it used primarily for content delivery only? Most writers use word processors, businesspeople routinely use spreadsheets, and draftsmen use computer-aided drawing tools to perform their daily work. It's not that manual processes are not available for these tasks but rather that these tools actively provide a better alternative than not using them. Despite the potential that many feel educational technology has in increasing the efficacy of instruction, technology has not yet provided a compelling enough alternative to the status quo.

Ralph Waldo Emerson once wrote, "Build a better mousetrap and the world will beat a path to your door." But it turns out that while having a better solution to a problem is necessary, it may not be sufficient to accomplish the goal. The rural sociologist Everett Rogers led a systematic study of ways innovations are introduced to and adopted by potential users, known as the *diffusion of innovations*. Many of the terms and concepts he identified, such as *laggards* and *early adopters*, have made their way into the language of business and popular culture. The diffusion of innovations provides a practical framework with which to study the common elements in such disparate areas as MTV marketing and animal husbandry.

In a series of diffusion studies across multiple areas, Rogers found that innovations that have higher levels of *high relative advantage* (a better mousetrap), *compatibility* (works well with what's available now), *trialability* (able to be personally tried), *observability* (can be seen in use), and *low complexity* (easy to use) are likely to succeed over innovations that possess lower levels of those attributes.[18] These factors are explored in more detail in later chapters, but it seems clear that earlier attempts at introducing technology into education fail to meet many of these requisites.

Educational technology, like most application domains, tends to be dependent on the larger technical, scientific, and theoretical environments it lives within. There are very few instances of the "tail wagging the dog" because of the high costs of developing technological infrastructure relative to the lower potential for recouping these investments in narrower markets. Therefore, innovations that are in sync with the environments they inhabit will tend to be more successful than ones that run counter to the trend.

K–12 education is fraught with ideological battles at all levels, from debates over content coverage and sources of funding to issues of assessment and the value of high-stakes testing. The many levels of institutional control—federal, state, county, and city—coupled with the often entrenched and contradictory positions of parents, teachers, and unions, make for an uneasy environment that resists change. Colleges have to contend with emerging issues of whether to accept credits earned in online courses delivered by other institutions and whether they themselves want to participate in the emerging global market for online education.

Technology by its very nature is constantly evolving. Those creating and promoting technology have strong incentives to introduce rapid changes, disrupting the marketplace to further their own interests, with little regard to the changes' effect on the overall infrastructure. By contrast, bureaucracies insulate schools from rapid change that may or may not stand the test of time. This mismatch is predominantly one of pacing and competing self-interests, and it provides some insight into technology's slow adoption in schools.

This is not to imply that the only motives for introducing technology into the classroom are economic. Parenthood often encourages professionals from varied fields to focus their efforts on education. B. F. Skinner was inspired to develop his teaching machine after a visit to his daughter's school, where he saw an opportunity to apply his work on learning from pigeons to children. Countless engineers, computer scientists, and other professionals have followed, seeking to make a difference by applying their domain expertise to what seems to be the unsolved problem of applying technology to education. My own reasons for wanting to get involved with educational technology stem from seeing a disconnect between what I knew technology to be capable of and its (still) largely unrealized potential for providing meaningful support for learning.

Classroom instruction is an expensive and time-consuming process, fraught with contradictory theories, motives, and frustratingly uneven results. The average cost to educate a student in U.S. K–12 schools rose more than 100 percent between 1995 and 2010.[19] The cost of higher education has been impressive as well, with the average college tuition rising 50 percent during the same period.[20] If these numbers were in line with inflation, or if the perceived increases in student learning even modestly tracked the costs, there would be far less public discourse about the rising costs of education, but the results are largely are flat, at least when measured by standardized tests.[21]

Economist and former Princeton University president William Bowen suggested that this disconnect might be explained by the idea of *cost disease*, when an industry or process is immune to increases in productivity over time.[22] Or, as Robert Frank puts it, "While productivity gains have made it possible to assemble cars with only a tiny fraction of the labor that was once required, it still takes four musicians nine minutes to perform Beethoven's String Quartet in C minor, just as it did in the nineteenth century."[23] To borrow a phrase from Internet parlance, education *doesn't scale*.

As fuzzy as educational research can often be, one fact is clear: the single most important factor in effective teaching is an effective teacher, one who is competent and engaging.[24] Many researchers suggest that the instructor's contribution is the largest factor in student success. But effective teaching is, unfortunately, an elusive quality, often described more as an art than a science. This has led policymakers to seek ways to "encourage" more effective teaching by using methods such as direct instruction,* high-stakes testing, strict control over the curricular content, pacing, and instructional technology.

Because the teacher's contribution is so considerable, it leaves very little opportunity for other ways to improve how students learn to have an effect. Techniques such as reducing class sizes, applying different pedagogical methodologies, offering psychological and societal interventions, and, germane to this book, utilizing technology ultimately will offer smaller potential for improvement in student learning.

Education is also subject to the whims of the educational or psychological theory of the moment. In the industrial era, schools were based on a factory model of education, and to a large extent they still are. The work of

---

Direct instruction is a teaching method in which teachers are given very explicit directions, even scripts, to guide the classroom activities moment by moment.

the progressive educators such as John Dewey and Jean Piaget after the turn of the twentieth-century was briefly popular until the behaviorist-inspired movements of John Watson and B. F. Skinner came to the fore. Behaviorism continued to dominate educational philosophy into the twenty-first century, with some incursions by constructivists, experiential learning techniques such as project- and problem-based learning and collaborative- and community-based learning.

Hard numbers on what schools actually spend on educational technology (excluding books) are difficult to come by, but according to a 2002 survey by the research data firm Quality Education Data (QED), U.S. schools spent $55 billion between 1991 and 2001. This figure typically includes all technology spending, including computers for administration as well as tools for teaching and learning. QED estimated that schools were spending an average of $97 per student per year directly on educational technology (hardware, software, support salaries, and training).[25] Multiplying that by the number of students in 2001 (approximately 60 million) suggests that current direct spending on educational technology in K–12 public schools is around $57 billion.[26] As of 2005, the United States had spent over $25 billion on providing schools with Internet access alone, not counting the equally impressive figure for hardware, software, and support personnel. So while there is much room for discussion about whether that money was wisely spent, it's clear that, whatever the actual number are, American schools have not resisted an investment in educational technology, but that investment does not appear to be having a meaningful effect on education.

The Role of Designers

Even the most rudimentary of technological devices was designed by a person, or a group of people, with the purpose of engaging the user in a kind of reflexive dialogue, however simplistic. This dialogue has features that encourage certain desired actions (*affordances*) and discourage unwanted actions (*constraints*).[27] The hornbooks of early America encouraged the learning of the alphabet by showing well-formed exemplars printed on the front. Upper and lowercase letters were separated to highlight their differences. Vowels and Roman numerals were arranged in separate rows and the horn casing discouraged "the innocent mischief resulting from damp and grubby paws."[28] This dance between affordances and constraints provides the bounds for interaction, making the device's designer a critical part of the pedagogical mix, along with the instructor and the learner.

At the risk of sounding the "this changes everything" alarm, I would argue that the modern personal computer is evolving into a very expressive medium designers of instructional technology can employ to engage in a more sophisticated dialogue with their learners. At a simple but incredibly useful level, the word processor I'm writing this on clues me in to my misspellings as I type by underscoring them with a wavy red line. Add to this local feedback the massive information people have made accessible on the Internet, and the dialogue includes not just the device's designers and individual contributions explicitly shared but a new form of collective "wisdom" algorithmically gleaned by statistically analyzing what many people do in multiple contexts, often referred to as "big data."

A good example is something most of us use every day: the Google search. If I'm interested in finding why my car's brakes are making growling sounds, I might type *sab break noyce*. Google will correct my misspellings and show results for *Saab brake noise*, which, aside from ads for new brake pads, will contain self-help forums where people have shared their experiences of how to deal with this problem.

The larger point here is that apart from being able to deftly deliver information based on simple search rules from a finite set of user-contributed pages, the system, by looking at how a many people searched for similar things, can infer that *sab* means *Saab* and not *sob* and that *break* refers to *brakes*. The new technologies of inference, big data, and natural language processing can provide designers of educational technology with unprecedented ability to create a reflexive dialogue with the learner on a level that simple mechanical tools are not capable of doing.

Should Technology Be Used in Education?

At the college level, the pressures of skyrocketing costs and competition from MOOCs and e-learning have made online educational technology a source of much discussion. Teresa Sullivan, the president of the University of Virginia, was summarily fired in a coup d'état in 2012 (and subsequently rehired because of protests from an outraged faculty and campus community) ostensibly because the university's governing board of visitors perceived her not to be embracing online education rapidly enough.

Most college students come to school equipped with a network-connected laptop computer and are provided by their institution with an email account and access to some sort of learning management system such as Blackboard or Sakai to provide academic content, receive class communications, and turn in assignments.

New York University media professor Clay Shirky makes a strong point that the college experience we fantasize for our children, where white-haired professors wearing leather-patched tweed jackets discuss literature in small seminars, is a reality only for a very small percentage of students at elite institutions. "The top 50 colleges on the *U.S. News and World Report* list (which includes most of the ones you've heard of) only educate something like 3 percent of the current student population."[29] The majority of students sit in impersonal classes with hundreds of other students to be lectured by instructors of varying competence, and they emerge from college with a degree plus often a crushing burden of debt. It is little wonder that the siren song of the new forms of technology-driven and potentially scalable forms of education such as e-learning* and MOOCs is resonating with some higher education leaders.

It is important to see some of the potentially threatening innovations such as MOOCs in the same way that their providers see them, as experiments. Daphne Koller, co-founder of venture-capital-funded MOOC developer Coursera, views the MOOC as an unprecedented opportunity to use the large numbers of people to scientifically test what works by doing controlled experiments she refers to as "A/B testing," where a change is made to instruction for some population of students and not for others. Because of the large numbers of students not typically available in traditional educational research, the results of the change can be tested empirically for its efficacy and the overall instruction changed accordingly.[30]

The answer is even less clear in K–12 education, where the students are younger and the habits of whole-class instruction are so entrenched. Teachers therefore have a much broader mission than college instructors do. Beyond delivering content for student absorption, teachers also have to establish learning skills and behavior management. Stanford University education professor Larry Cuban lists the contradictory messages that

---

E-learning is a name attached to many Internet-based technologies that allow students to engage with instruction remotely.

come from the people and institutions that set policies, routines, and expectations for K–12 classrooms:

- Socialize all children, yet nourish each child's creativity.
- Teach the best the past has to offer, but ensure that each child possesses practical skills marketable in the community.
- Demand obedience to authority, but prepare children to compete.[31]

Clearly, students need to be prepared to use the technological tools of their generation; today that means the computer or tablet. But the successful introduction of technology in whole-class instruction does not easily fit the teaching methods currently employed in most U.S. schools. The majority of K–12 schools do not provide students with laptops or encourage them to use them in the classroom. When they do, students are disruptively herded into computer labs, or carts filled with laptops are wheeled in for specific curricular activities. The use of individual computers makes teachers less willing to introduce technology into their classrooms because it interferes with the whole-class nature of current instructional practice. Contrast this with the almost uniform adoption of digital projectors and "smart boards," which evolved directly from the last generation of education technology, the film projector and the chalkboard.

Finally, there is a huge potential for technology to enable learners not enrolled in a formal educational institution to access a wealth of instructional material through the Internet. For example, those taking advantage of the latest Internet-based learning tools, MOOCs, turn out to be a fairly diverse group, with a mean age of thirty-seven years; over 77 percent of them reside outside of the United States, and over 81 percent already having a college degree.[32] Because only a handful of universities accept MOOCs for course credit, and very few, if any, K–12 schools do so, we can assume that the majority of learners are taking these often time-consuming classes to increase their personal learning.

Some Cautious Optimism

In spite of the challenges outlined above, I am still cautiously hopeful about the use of computers in education for K–12 and beyond. This is an exciting time in terms of the technologies and infrastructure available to build ever more capable tools that can help learning in any number of areas, including whole-class instructional support, individual inquiry, and project-based learning to a whole new generation of online learning tools.

Computer-based technology continues to improve at a pace that eclipses the more mechanical technologies that preceded it. In 1965, Gordon Moore, co-founder of microprocessor giant Intel, predicted that microprocessors would double in capability every 18 months, while costing the same.[33] Moore's Law has held true for almost fifty years, and it has enabled computers to get faster, more capable, or cheaper (pick whichever dimension is important to the problem you want to solve) at rates that enable innovative solutions to problems that were impossible just a short time earlier.

The rapid adoption of the Internet has made it an invaluable repository of the world's intellectual output. Institutions such as the Library of Congress have made millions of historical records and documents available. Individuals assembling their family's genealogy have uploaded and connected family trees. Libraries, Google Books, and the new Digital Public Library of America have digitized countless books. Individual scholars have posted a wealth of articles. And don't forget the thousands of videos of cats playing the piano.

Connections to that ever more robust Internet have become ubiquitous and fast. According to the Pew Foundation, over 78 percent of American adults connected to the Internet in 2011, and over 62 percent of them did so with a fast broadband connection.[34] This increased access and speed has enabled a new class of Web-based application that instantly connects us with Web resources at a very granular level to rapidly construct meaningful and personalized views of those data. The community-based ethos that harnessed that connectivity has helped produce useful resources such as Wikipedia and open-source software such as Linux and Apache, which in turn have allowed software developers to build upon each other's efforts to create tools that are bigger than one individual or company can create alone. And now a majority of learners carry in their pocket a personally addressable Internet-connected computer workstation that would have made computer engineers in the 1980s sigh with envy at its power, a fact that offers endless possibilities to makers of the next generation of teaching machines.

Of course, a better mousetrap alone will not compel educators to adopt the latest innovations, any more than the state-of-the-art of innovations from previous generations of teaching machines did. It is my hope that looking critically at the past will help us avoid some of the adoption hurdles and provide educators and learners useful tools that facilitate student learning in an engaging, effective, and economical manner.

What Is a Teaching Machine?

It's clear that educational technology has meant different things at different times. From the blackboard to Blackboard.com, the kind of educational technology offered reflects its environment; as theorists proffer new conceptions about how people learn, the capabilities of the base technology grow ever most sophisticated and affordable, and people clamor to provide automated solutions to teaching problems. For the purposes of this book it is necessary to limit the scope of what will be explored in any depth. I can appreciate the hornbook's place in the history of educational technology, but its simplicity necessarily limits its instructive value provide guidance in the technology-driven the world where we now live.

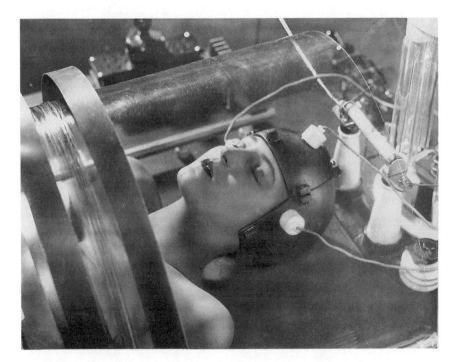

Figure 1.4. A frame from Fritz Lang's film, *Metropolis* (1927).

For my purposes in this book, a *teaching machine* is defined as a way to deliver instruction by using technology that marries content and pedagogy into a self-directed experience for a learner and which relies on minimal assistance from a live instructor. The notion of what is a machine needs to be taken more broadly so it can include less mechanical devices such as programmed instructional textbooks but not other, equally valuable but less content-driven, innovations such as graphing calculators. In this definition, a book can be teaching machine but not a blackboard and not even the new electronic smart boards, in spite of their highly sophisticated electronics and obvious usefulness in whole-class instruction.

In some sense, the title of this book is meant to poke fun at the industrial age ideas of education and fears about the mechanization of schools, as depicted in Fritz Lang's 1927 dystopian film *Metropolis* (figure 1.4), in which students are treated like automobiles being assembled in a factory by robots. While it may seem that some educational technology proponents adhere to this notion, the teaching machine has the potential to do just the opposite: to be a student-centered tool that encourages the dreams Pestalozzi had over two centuries ago.

2

Sage on the Stage

A half-century ago, the media theorist Marshall McLuhan famously observed that new types of media initially replicate the forms that preceded them until they can establish themselves as a medium that exploits their unique features. The first movies were little more than films of dramatic stage plays. The first attempts at using teaching machines tended to follow this pattern, with various methods (the postal service, radio, television, and film) delivering content in the same form as the media of the past.[1]

The phrase "sage on the stage, guide on the side" refers to an expression commonly used in education that highlights the difference between lecture-driven instruction, where a central figure possessing all the knowledge transmits it for passive students to absorb, and more constructivist approaches, where learners construct knowledge by making sense of new information.[2]

This chapter looks at correspondence courses, which replicated textbooks, and examines educational films, radio, and television, which sought to reproduce the experience of the classroom lecture. Most recently, the Internet has proven to be a more capable delivery mechanism for media-based educational methods, but the pattern remains the same. The current providers of these media tend to feature an instructor lecturing to passive learners, albeit in smaller chunks of ten to twenty minutes.

All these teaching methods follow the same didactic style of instruction familiar from our own and our children's educational experiences. The instructor, who presumably possesses valuable content knowledge, packages that information into smaller portions, called lessons, and delivers these for students to passively absorb and hopefully understand. The extent of that understanding is verified through assessments, such as quizzes, tests, and essays.

The stories of the Chautauqua movement and the commercial correspondence schools can help us understand current efforts in distance education, including today's MOOCs. These earlier ventures proved that they could cost-effectively deliver instruction anytime anywhere using the technology available—in their case, the U.S. Postal Service. To borrow a concept from the Internet age, they were able to scale.*

Correspondence Courses

In the nineteenth century, Americans looked for ways to educate themselves other than in formal settings such as colleges, as higher education was available to only a small percentage of the population. As the industrial revolution unfolded, skilled workers sought ways to separate themselves from less-skilled ones and to make themselves competitive in a crowded labor force. These needs tended to be more pragmatic than the loftier goals of universities. Commercial entities sprang up to fill the void, and a new kind of distance-education tool was born: the correspondence course.

The correspondence schools offered instruction through textbooks mailed using the newly created rural free delivery (RFD) service, which made it possible to send and receive mail in a timely fashion to even the most remote rural areas. Students responded with essays and completed examinations. They often asked specific questions, which were answered by return mail. Upon successful completion of the course, they typically received a certificate of completion.[3]

Chautauqua Literary and Scientific Circle

The first large-scale correspondence courses came from a most unlikely source: the Chautauqua movement, which helped Americans in the post–Civil War transition as "the center of gravity shifted from farm and counting-house to factory and mine."[4] The movement grew out of a site located in a beautiful part of southwestern New York State, on Lake Chautauqua, and initially used in the 1870s by the Methodist church for evangelical

---

*The ability to scale refers to an Internet company being able to serve an ever-increasing audience without having major technological problems or incurring large expenses that makes the enterprise insolvent.

Figure 2.1. The Oriental House, Chautauqua, New York.
From A. Hyde, *The Story of Methodism* (Greenfield, MA: Wiley, 1897)

"camp-meetings." It then evolved into a nonsectarian intellectual, literary, and musical retreat that exists to this day (figure 2.1). The historian Joe Kett described the Chautauqua as "a Disneyland for culture."[5]

In 1874, John Heyl Vincent, a Methodist minister and editor of the *Sunday School Journal* in Akron, Ohio, and Lewis Miller, a businessman active in his church (and Thomas Edison's son-in-law), were charged with finding a location for a two-week summer institute to train Bible school teachers. Both had been active in trying to reform the Sunday school curriculum to appeal to a wider group of Christians than just Methodists. They had already begun to provide printed and graded lesson materials that ventured beyond simple Bible stories to include geography and history—and later, even science.[6] Vincent was inclined to seek an urban location for the institute, but Miller successfully persuaded him, using "amiable assistance and cogent argument" to choose the idyllic campground on the banks of Lake Chautauqua.[7]

The initial summer institute was a success, and the Chautauqua Assembly was formed to train Sunday school teachers in a progressive manner, with Vincent saying, "I gave it the name of 'Assembly' to distinguish it from ordinary Sunday School institutes and conventions."[8] Miller and Vincent would continue to work closely together until Vincent's retirement in 1902, with Miller acting as the president of Chautauqua, presiding over the business aspects, while Vincent took the role of superintendent of education, overseeing the intellectual and cultural direction.[9]

The Chautauqua Assembly quickly evolved from a Methodist religious school to a more secular annual retreat for culture and learning. During the summers, concerts and plays were held in the beautiful open-air venues, and there were distinguished participants, including President Ulysses S. Grant in 1875. But the overall emphasis was on education, with a college of liberal arts and several internal schools dedicated to language learning, theology, and teacher education. Speeches from the leading orators of the time, including William Jennings Bryan and Theodore Roosevelt, were common; even the venerable National Education Association met at Chautauqua, in 1880.[10]

John Heyl Vincent (figure 2.2) was born in Alabama in 1832 and began his working life in the Methodist church as an itinerant minister, known as a circuit rider. Not unlike Abraham Lincoln's early career as a prairie lawyer, Vincent traveled from town to town serving rural churches where the populations could not support a resident minister. This wandering lifestyle in the Pennsylvania hill country kept Vincent from attending college, something he regretted his entire life.[11]

After the Civil War, Vincent fulfilled his lifelong ambition of improving religious instruction and was put in charge of the church's Sunday School Union. In 1868 he became editor of the *Sunday School Journal* and a publisher of books on religious instruction. Up to that point, most churches had put little effort into the pedagogy of religious instruction, and curriculum was developed locally. Vincent changed that in 1870 when he introduced the Bercan System of Lessons. These lessons were systematically designed with "skillful markings to arrest attention" and illustrations; he published them as columns in his journal, and they became a big success internationally.[12]

As a Methodist minister, John Vincent was an improbable leader of such a progressive educational and cultural experiment. The early American Methodists were poor and uneducated, and did not place much value in a liberal education, to the point that some even opposed the Sunday schools because they violated the sanctity of the Sabbath. Vincent was against the fundamentalist faction of the religious, who used big camp meetings to

Figure 2.2. John Heyl Vincent, 1890.
Chautauqua Institution Archives, Oliver Archives Center

proselytize. Saying that they "can be very trying," he quietly sought to marginalize the participation of the more evangelical members from the Chautauqua and thought of the church as "a large school dedicated to Christian education."[13]

Thankfully for Vincent, Methodism already had a more intellectual side because of its founder's influence. John Wesley, the denomination's founder, was an Oxford graduate who spoke several languages, was broadly read across disciplines, and wrote over 400 titles, many of them secular, such as his 1753 *The Complete English Dictionary*. The American Methodist branch started its own publishing house in 1789 and printed many short and inexpensive religious educational pamphlets, which it encouraged all of its circuit riders to read for at least five hours a day. In 1818, the church further affirmed its commitment to education, and presaging Vincent's later interest in distance learning, it required any circuit rider wishing to attend the national conference to pass a two-year course of home study.[14]

Of particular interest to the topic of this book was the founding of the Chautauqua Literary and Scientific Circle (CLSC), which would become the first sustained experiment in distance learning in America. The CSLC started in 1878 with 500 "readers" who desired to "promote the habits of study and reading in connection to the routine of daily life." These participants were organized in circles based on their home locations, and they met in person at Lake Chautauqua during the summer, reading on their own throughout the rest of the year, much like modern executive MBA programs. Instructors distributed questions for each book, and students were expected to provide written responses, which would be corrected and returned to them. Students unable to get in-person feedback to their answers mailed them to the Chautauqua and received a response by return mail.[15]

A full CLSC program took four years to complete, after which the participants would receive a diploma at an elaborate ceremony called a "recognition day." Each year was dedicated to a single subject, consisting of either English, American, continental European, or classical topics. The CLSC organizers sold textbooks and even wrote their own adaptations and abridgements of classics to make their lengths more digestible, noting, "Every line in Green's *Short History* is interesting, but after all, there's a good deal of it." All the adaptations were fully vetted by academics to instill "the reverence properly felt for any piece of writing that drops from the pen of a professor."[16]

In 1882, the *Chautauqua Assembly Herald* proclaimed the program to be "the first systematic plan for correspondence instruction formally announced in this country."[17] The CSLC grew in popularity, with over 750,000 readers by 1912.[18] Participants came from a great variety of sources: teacher associations, YMCAs, YWCAs, Native American schools, and even prisons. To manage these numbers, CSLC organizers developed an elaborate system of book distribution, using the fledgling postal service as well as independent shipping companies. To support the readers, CSLC began publishing an inexpensive newsletter, *The Chautauquan*, in 1890; its first editor was Ida Tarbell, before her career as a muckraking journalist. *The*

Chautauquan offered a wide range of tips on speech and manners, study guidance, and practical advice from Bishop John Vincent himself.[19]

Distance education has a long history of less than admirable completion rates, when compared with in-person forms of education. In 1906, the largest of the commercial correspondence schools had an incredibly low 2.6 percent of its students completing any given course.[20] Modern online schools such as Capella University and the University of Phoenix have dramatically lower retention rates as compared with on-site schooling, often less than 50 percent.[21] In this grand tradition, MOOCs, too, have very low completion rates, often in the single digits, because of their low- or no-cost tuitions and instant access.[22] The CLSC was no exception, reporting 12 percent completion rate in the programs during 1891.[23]

The Chautauqua Literary and Scientific Circle provided a well-publicized and useful model for correspondence courses in traditional academia, as well as in the commercial sectors, to follow. Some paths were quite direct. William Rainey Harper left teaching at a Baptist theological seminary in 1883 to join the Chautauqua faculty. He quickly rose through the ranks, becoming the head of the College of Liberal Arts. In 1891, the industrialist John D. Rockefeller selected Harper as the first president of the University of Chicago, where he initiated many of the innovations that Chautauqua championed: summer schools, correspondence study, and university extension classes.

International Correspondence Schools

Following the tradition set by the Chautauqua movement, the International Correspondence Schools (ICS) in Scranton, Pennsylvania, became the largest and most successful school for distance education. The ICS was founded by Thomas Foster in 1891 to teach safety procedures to Pennsylvania coal miners. The offerings soon expanded to cover hundreds of subjects. Classes typically relied on booklets of custom curricula, requiring the learners to send in their assignments by return mail. By 1926, more than 2.5 million students had taken one or more of its courses.[24]

Thomas J. Foster (figure 2.3) was born in 1843, in a small town just south of Scranton. After serving in the Union Army during the Civil War, he worked as a printer near Scranton. The economy of central Pennsylvania was heavily driven by the emerging coal industry, with hundreds of mines

Figure 2.3. Thomas J. Foster, founder of the International Correspondence Schools.
ICS Collection, Weinberg Memorial Library, University of Scranton

in the area; but the working and safety conditions in these mines led to the deaths or injuries of hundreds of mine workers.

Foster grew upset at these needless tragedies, which reached a peak when a fire at the Avondale mine killed 192 workers in 1869. That year, Foster left the printing business and started a newspaper to address mine-safety issues. He believed the primary cause of these disasters was the mine foremen's lack of education about mining science and machinery. He also may have seen a good business opportunity in the making. His biweekly *Shenandoah Herald*, focusing on mine issues, went daily in 1875.[25]

In response to the Avondale fire and other mining disasters, the Pennsylvania State Legislature passed the Mine Safety Act of 1885, which required miners and inspectors to pass exhaustive examinations on mine safety. Unfortunately, these tests proved confusing to the relatively uneducated mine workers, and they struggled to pass them so they could remain employed by the mines. No continuing-education institutions were available to provide support for working miners.[26]

Responding to the need, Foster instituted a question-and-answer column in his paper, later called a "correspondence column," to help miners pass the safety exams. He asked readers to write letters with questions and problems about the examinations, and he and his staff would answer them in the newspaper. He even printed old copies of the state exams, along with the answers to help test-takers study. When the newspaper was quickly overwhelmed with the volume of questions, Foster, seizing the moment, looked for a more scalable solution. He recognized that the miners needed education in foundational subjects such a basic math as well as in technical mining, saying, "Teach a man the basics, and that man can apply those principles to any situation."[27]

In 1890, Foster founded the predecessor of the International Correspondence Schools as a one-year residential program, enrolling 500 miners in Scranton. He soon recognized that many potential students found it difficult to take a full year off from their jobs, and many others were unable to travel to Scranton to attend in person. Ever the astute businessman, Foster began to offer home-study courses using the postal system the following year. He adapted the residential course into a collection of short lessons on specific subjects, which were printed as pamphlets and mailed to the students. The students would send back written responses, which were corrected and returned.[28]

By breaking down the curriculum into very small parts that moved by small steps, the ICS courses "put the teacher into the text."[29] This process established a pacing that presaged the successive approximation approach Skinner and his fellow behaviorists would use decades later in their teaching machines. ICS texts were clearly written, using simple language that did not require the kinds of knowledge a typical college student might already possess but which the average mine worker typically did not. Foster estimated that 90 percent of his students were unable to work fractions, so he built remedial instruction into some of the lessons or else encouraged students to add a basic math class his course offerings.[30]

One of the reasons for ICS's success was Foster's understanding of the students he served and an insistence on putting their needs forefront. The average learner was 27 years old, worked in a coal mine, and had a family to support. The student would study at home and "use the kitchen table as a desk, and often rock the cradle with one hand to keep baby quiet, while holding the lesson paper in the other."[31] The educational goals were finely focused, as an ICS executive explained: "The regular technical school or college aims to educate a man broadly; our aim, on the contrary, is to educate him only along some particular line."[32]

This idea of providing learning any place, any time is as important to modern distance-education learners as it was to early-twentieth-century coal miners. The ability to detach time and space constraints from education is perhaps the biggest reason why people enroll in Internet-based e-learning offerings; the courses allow them to participate without interfering with their work commitments. The most common approach today is *asynchronous* learning, in which students in different places access the lectures and resources whenever it is most convenient for them. *Synchronous* learning experiences occur when students are physically in different locations but "meet" online at the same time.

The ICS provided instruction in 50-page lessons in leather-bound textbooks, called "Instruction and Questions Papers," with approximately 100 lessons making up any given course. Each lesson would end with a review of 10–15 questions that required free-format answers, written in longhand. The ICS textbooks were similar in content and scope to those used in colleges, but the language used was simpler and more accessible. College textbooks were seen as having too much extraneous material and requiring "too great a knowledge about mathematics and other subjects." In total, the ICS texts covering the same topic were typically half the length of college textbooks, and they attempted to demystify industrial technology and science.[33]

The ICS courses were rigorous, both in terms of the content and the homework required. The coal mine safety class required the student to write over 117,000 words and draw 83 diagrams in response to the questions accompanying the instruction. Students took a varying amount of time to complete the full course, ranging from 10 months to 13 years, 2 months.[34]

The ICS took the students' answers to the Instruction and Questions Papers very seriously. Foster believed that without assistance, "it is not expected that many students will pass the final examinations and receive diplomas."[35] With a 200:1 student-to-faculty ratio,[36] ICS applied Taylor-esque mass-production techniques to correct student assignments. Foster described "scores of women sitting five abreast at desks checked the student work in assembly line fashion, who turned it over to instructors to double check." Poor work was returned to the student to do over and then was re-corrected.[37]

The grading in all correspondence schools often was "over generous," resulting in less than mastery-level learning. The integrity of the students' assignments was subject to an honor system, and there is little evidence that many students violated this trust.[38] If students had trouble, special instructors were assigned to help them. All incoming questions were carefully answered, even those asking for information outside the scope of the course.[39] The issue of authenticating student responses persists in the current e-learning products, where new technology is being developed to validate student identities remotely.[40]

With the success of the mining course, ICS branched out to form 31 separate sub-schools, teaching subjects as diverse as architecture, chemistry, civil service exam preparation, and window dressing. All subjects were taught through hundreds of specifically targeted small courses that could be mixed to create truly customized programs of study. The school kept close ties with industries whose workers it was training, and it was popular with employers.[41]

Educational experiences imply a trust relationship between student and instructor, not unlike a doctor-patient relationship. Both the patient and the student need to trust that the doctor and instructor have their best interests at heart. The introduction of money into the mix often complicates this trust. Whatever altruistic intentions were behind Thomas Foster's initial motivation to help teach mine safety, he unabashedly saw ICS as a business that sold a product to customers. He said in 1906, "This is a commercial enterprise. It is necessarily so." But he added, "The business is conducted for gain, but with gain as the motive influencing his teacher, the student fares as well as when he is the beneficiary of the state." As a business, correspondence school was very capital intensive, with the plates for printing the textbooks costing over $1.5 million ($300–800 million in today's dollars).[42]

The ICS initially relied on advertising that appealed to the Horatio Alger–inspired dream of upward mobility through hard work and determi-

Figure 2.4. Early International Correspondence Schools advertisement (1905). ICS Collection, Weinberg Library, University of Scranton

nation. ICS "preached the relationship between education and success" and used over $2 million in advertising by 1916 to tell the company story.[43] A 1905 ad offers the opportunity to move from a "man" to a "manager," rhetorically asking, "On which side of the desk are you?" (figure 2.4). The ad foreshadows Florence Reese's famous 1931 organized labor song "Which

Side Are You On?" by saying, "The man before the desk works with his hands and is paid for his *labor*, while the man behind the desk works with his head and is paid for his *knowledge*." In 1906, ICS added a large direct sales force to augment its advertising.[44]

The ICS courses were not inexpensive, costing around $110 in 1906 (about three months' salary), and they were usually purchased on an installment plan of $5 to $10 per month. This presented an opportunity for ICS, in that students could take classes without having the full tuition in advance, and ICS made additional revenue from the 18 percent interest rate it charged. But this payment method also presented a problem because of the very low completion rates.[45] ICS's 2.6 percent completion rate was dismal, even in an industry where the average completion rate was only 6 percent.[46]

The ICS was keenly aware of this "delinquency" issue. An ICS executive lamented in 1906, "We have absolutely no way of compelling a student to study."[47] Many students took part in this installment program, but they stopped paying if they stopped learning; so ICS took steps to address the problem with things they *could* do. The school allowed students to transfer to different classes for $1 fee, and a large staff of dedicated salesmen, known as the "Encouragement Department," wrote over 15,000 letters to struggling students by 1906. Salespeople were given the same sales commission for redeeming a delinquent student as for recruiting a new one.[48]

Lessons from the Chautauqua and Correspondence Courses

The developers of today's e-learning efforts would be wise to pay attention to the issues that the Chautauqua movement and commercial correspondence schools actively struggled with a century earlier. Many of the same problems remain: how to keep students engaged, effectively deliver content from a distance, provide a rigorous but still accessible curriculum, offer meaningful and timely feedback, foster a community of learners, and most critically, scale to meet the demands of large numbers of users.

The Chautauqua movement provided a good model for the commercial correspondence schools and university extension schools that followed. Its organizers developed curricula specific to the needs of distant learners, and they created a strategy for deploying content using the postal service. The CSLC reading circles provided a framework for students to feel connected with the school. The annual meetings at Lake Chautauqua helped cement those bonds and were the forerunners of the modern-day online forums and meet-ups* that many e-learning providers offer.

This issue of low completion rates in correspondence school programs (and MOOCs) probably should not be judged against completion rates in traditional classrooms, since the rewards for completion may be different. In the traditional classroom, students are rewarded for completion by receiving credits toward a degree, whereas students in correspondence courses are more often seeking specific knowledge and may quit once they have gained it. In the case of the Pennsylvania coal miners, their goal was to pass the state-required examination; once that happened, they had no reason to continue paying Mr. Foster $5–10 per month for a certificate.

The educator Carol Tomlinson has advocated a pedagogical philosophy known as "differentiated instruction," in which instructors try to meet students where they are, in terms of general abilities and existing knowledge, and teach from there.[49] ICS used a similar strategy, providing textbooks that did not assume prior knowledge and were written in an accessible language and style and creating individualized courses from a large collection of smaller classes. The result was a differentiated and better learning experience for the student.

Thomas Foster was not afraid to admit that ICS was in business to make money, and the company successfully straddled the line between academic rigor and revenue. Those who ran ICS saw students as their customers, and they offered true value in return for money. They provided timely and meaningful feedback on student assignments, and they organized measures to lessen the burden on instructors.

Finally, correspondence schools successfully scaled to support vast numbers of students, using the resources that were available during the period. They did this through understanding their students and providing a back-end infrastructure that could support an effective bi-directional conversation, albeit a slow one, with thousands of students simultaneously.

Educational Film

In the spirit of Marshall McLuhan's observations on media, correspondence schools replicated the textbook, and "talking heads" educational

---

Meet-ups are face-to-face meetings arranged by local members of larger online learning groups to meet locally and discuss issues from the class.

film, radio, and television replicated the classroom lecture. The allure was one of economy of scale; produce an episode at a fixed cost and then present that experience over and over, presumably at a lower incremental cost each time, in contrast to a live instructor who must constantly deliver the lecture at the same cost per performance. Today's MOOCs and e-learning efforts tug at the same fantasy: record the lectures of professors from elite universities once, and deliver them to a grateful audience worldwide, sometimes with thousands of students.

Of course not all media are lecture-based, and educational film tended to follow the model of the theater and entertainment industry more than the classroom. Educational films pioneered the idea of "edutainment," productions that offered educational content with a more engaging presentation style. Even though the inventors of the motion picture originally envisioned film as an educational medium, it was primarily used for entertainment until a large enough collection of specifically produced titles became available in the 1910s and schools began to purchase projectors for classroom use. Thomas Edison was so enthralled with the potential of educational film that in 1913 he said, "Books will soon be obsolete in our schools . . . Our school system will be completely changed in ten years."[50]

Strictly speaking, traditional educational film is not really a teaching machine, according to my definition. While films clearly use technology to deliver educational content, teachers typically used them to supplement traditional instruction rather than to provide primary instruction. I will briefly discuss them because they played an important role in establishing the need to develop infrastructure to support educational technology in the classroom, and also because of their later role in funding other teaching machines.

The first educational films were inspired by the newsreels that ran in movie theaters before the start of the feature. These newsreels were very short clips that highlighted current events throughout the world with a narrated overview; to this day, newsreels provide documentary filmmakers with a wealth of historic footage. The early educational films used outtakes from these newsreels and cast-offs from other commercial film projects to create short educational subjects. George Kleine created the first catalog dedicated to educational film in 1910, with over 1,000 titles in 30 subjects Thomas Edison created a series of films on nature and physical science starting in 1911 and ending in 1914 when a fire destroyed many of the negatives.[51]

The use of film in the classroom was hampered by the technology of film itself. In 1910, Kleine tried to convince the New York City public schools to adopt his educational films, but despite strong support from the board of education, there was a lack of venues and equipment to project them.[52] Commercial film used a large 35mm width that required heavy and bulky projectors and the film was expensive to use, requiring hefty 14-inch reels holding 1,000 feet to play only 11 minutes. A smaller, 16mm-gauge film was developed in 1912, and manufacturers began making less expensive and more portable projectors to fit the new compact sized film. The 16mm film was also more economical, requiring only 400 feet on a smaller 7-inch reel to play the same 11 minutes as compared to the wider stock.

Size was not the only issue. Films were made of an extremely flammable cellulous-nitrate plastic, and strict safety laws were enacted to protect viewers so that schools would never be able to show these films in the classroom. In 1922, Eastman Kodak introduced an acetate-based "safety film" that was more fireproof.[53] During college, I worked at the National Archives converting Universal Newsreels from nitrate to safety film and, because the statute of limitations has presumably lapsed, can personally attest to nitrate's volatility. During lunch one day, we lit a one-inch strip of discarded film in the parking lot. It burned fiercely like phosphorus for several minutes, refusing to be extinguished with water or stamping on it. Nitrate film could also spontaneously combust. A massive explosion at one of the National Archives' storage buildings in 1978 in Maryland leveled the structure and destroyed over 13-million feet of historic footage.[54]

Some of the first films were produced by the makers of projectors: Kodak, Victor, Bell & Howell, and AT&T (through its manufacturing arm, Western Electric). As the "talkies" began to overtake silent pictures, Electrical Research Products Inc. (ERPI) began to produce sound films for education. In a bid to add some academic credibility to their films, they began an alliance with the University of Chicago in 1932.[55] Anti-trust pressure on AT&T from the US Justice Department caused ERPI to be sold to the popular Encyclopaedia Britannica in 1937. The largest producer and distributor of educational films was Encyclopaedia Britannica Films (which would later play a role in the 1960s teaching machines era). Britannica also had a close relationship with the University of Chicago, and, in 1941, it was acquired by the university. Ever the savvy marketer, the president of Encyclopaedia Britannica changed the name from ERPI to Encyclopaedia Britannica Films, after overhearing a middle-school student pronounce the name as "burpy."[56]

Educational Radio

It would be easy to dismiss educational radio as a failed experiment in trying to harness the technology of the day for education, only to be superseded by the next best thing, but the story is a bit more nuanced. Radio turned out not to be particularly effective in urban schools, but it provided outreach to rural classrooms that, not unlike some schools in today's rural America, lacked the range of faculty able to teach a broad curriculum. It also later provided an opportunity for students to take an active role in producing instructional programs themselves.[57]

In the mid-1920s, public school systems in the Midwest and a few colleges and universities began experimenting with using radio. Efforts proved ineffective because professors simply lectured into a microphone, and it became evident that the skills of a good lecturer did not necessarily qualify one as an effective broadcaster.[58]

After years of missionary work with the Country Life Institute and after graduating from the agricultural extension of the Maryland State College, Benjamin H. ("Uncle Ben") Darrow (figure 2.5) was put in charge of the children's programs at WLS radio, the Sears-Roebuck owned commercial station in Chicago, in 1924. At WLS, Darrow piloted a show called *The Little Red School House of the Air*, which broadcast lessons in art, music appreciation, and geography. Each episode wove dialogue and music around a particular topic, all written and performed by students and their teachers who would rehearse using dummy microphones at school and then broadcast from the studio the programs at set times each week. These programs were very well received by both rural and city schools throughout the Chicago listening area.[59]

Darrow had aspirations to be an inventor; after the Little Red School House, he decided to take some years off to patent and market the TABL-TUB, which was a cross between a kitchen sink and a bathtub that was never successful.[60] He filed another patent in 1947, this time for a classroom globe that, instead of pivoting on the north and south poles, used an

Figure 2.5. Educational radio pioneer Benjamin H. Darrow, ca. 1931.
Courtesy Ohio State University Photo Archive

elaborate support system so the earth was cradled within to eliminate wear and tear.[61] Uncle Ben was more successful as an educational radio producer and advocate than as an itinerant inventor.

Darrow's experience with the *Little Red School House of the Air* solidified his sense of the potential impact radio might have on education and it led him on a Sisyphean crusade to gain support for other instructional radio programs. Ben Darrow saw radio as a global village, where "the voice of the world becomes one neighborhood." He succeeded in establishing a number of other successful "School of the Air" programs throughout the country, including the *Wisconsin School of the Air*,* which was on the air for over 40 years.[62]

In the 1950s, a number of researchers studied the effectiveness of instruction by radio and generally concluded that there were few or no gains over traditional teaching techniques.[63] (These kinds of results are typical when researchers compare one method of delivering instruction to another.) Instruction by radio may also have suffered from its focus on a single sense, hearing. Even in a lecture, the visual presence of the speaker can communicate far more information than the sound alone, with facial and hand gestures, not to mention writing on the blackboard, which contributes much to the communicative experience. I am a big consumer of recorded books, and I listen to many podcasts a week, but there are not many times I listen without performing some other activity, such as walking or driving. Sitting in the classroom and passively listening to radio broadcasts may have seemed exciting at first but ultimately was not an immersive enough experience for students to embrace.

Educational Television

America saw an incredibly rapid growth in the purchase of television sets, starting in the 1950s, when there were only a few thousand TVs, to well over 50 million a decade later. The U.S. government and the Ford Foundation's Fund for the Enhancement of Education (which would also fund B. F. Skinner's teaching machines in the 1960s) each spent over $100 million during the 1960s for classroom trials of educational television in over 250 school systems and 50 colleges throughout the United States, involving over 300,000 students.[64]

The academic results of these trials were mildly encouraging, showing relatively small increases over traditional classroom teaching, but the main reason advocates pushed educational television was its potential ability to scale one-time production costs over a larger audience and to transform

---

*My editor offered this anecdote: "When I was in grad. school in Madison I met a dairy farmer who told me this was all he would play on the radio in his milking parlor— that the cows loved it." Greg Britton, personal communication, September 9, 2013.

education from a labor-intensive and expensive affair into one that could be manufactured and brought to scale. A Ford Foundation report calculated the break-even point where televised lessons became cost effective over traditional classroom instruction to be a mere 200–220 students, suggesting that educational television could be a very cost-effective way to educate students.[65]

But using television to deliver education introduced new problems. Classes needed to be closely synchronized with the broadcasters, and each broadcast channel could air only one lesson at a time. One particularly inventive solution in 1961 involved the use of airplanes equipped with television transmitters that constantly hovered at 23,000 feet over a number of central Indiana schools, beaming videotaped instruction to them at agreed-upon times.[66]

Educational television proffered a new definition of "team teaching." Instead of two teachers presenting in the classroom, this type of team teaching paired the classroom teacher with a studio teacher who taught for 20 to 30 minutes each day and who came prepared with the lesson plans. As an added benefit, the classroom teacher could spend more time with students individually. This idea is a forerunner of what is being called the flipped classroom, in which students watch instructional videos on the Internet on their own time and spend their time in class interacting with, rather than being lectured to by, the teacher.[67]

Educational Television in American Samoa

American Samoa is about as unlikely a place for the most ambitious implementation of educational television that one could imagine. But the idyllic island in the South Pacific, about 2,500 miles south of Hawaii, was host to a "bold experiment" in education during the 1960s and 1970s.[68] As daring as the experiment was, it was also a textbook example of how *not* to introduce educational technology into a school system, with an American Samoan governor calling it an "utter failure" during a congressional hearing in 1970.[69]

The island of Samoa became an American territory in 1899, as part of a deal with Germany following some naval squabbles between the Germany and the United States; prior to that, it had been strategic as a coal refueling station for shipping and whaling.[70] The island was initially governed by a series of U.S. Navy governors, then by politically appointed civilian governors whose average tenure was less then a year until President Kennedy appointed H. Rex Lee as governor in 1961.

Hyrum Rex Lee was born in Idaho in 1910, earned his degree in agricultural economics at the age of 26, and began working in various government agencies, including the Department of Agriculture, the Bureau of Indian Affairs, and the infamous War Relocation Authority responsible for the internment of Japanese-Americans during World War II.[71] When Lee and his family arrived in American Samoa in 1961, he found an educational system in chaos. Students were taught in rural one-room schools by teachers who did not have any formal training in education. Not a single teacher had a teaching certificate, and none tested beyond the 5th-grade level. Samoan teachers often spent the first two months of each school year catching students up from the previous year's studies.[72] Decades of military leadership and short-term governors with reorganization plans that changed from year to year left the educational system in a dismal state, with one Samoan educational leader lamenting, "We have not been able to make as much progress as countries with less experience and less money. Perhaps the most important thing of all would be continuity."[73] Rex Lee brought that continuity to American Samoa, staying six years and carrying out a stable set of educational reforms.

Lee pondered a number of solutions to the educational morass he encountered, including the hiring of 300 mainland teachers to replace the Samoans; but he rejected this because of the high cost of relocating these teacher and paying their higher salaries. He could train the Samoan teachers, but he decided that would take too long. "Television, it seemed to me," Lee remarked, "might be a way to bring about a quick upgrading of the educational system of our islands and an upgrading of the Samoan teachers at the same time."[74] Lee already was positively predisposed toward educational television. In the states, his daughter had learned how to touch type from an educational television program and was promptly offered an office job. Lee, impressed by her success, enrolled in and completed a conversational French language television course.[75] Invoking speed and drama as his guiding principles, Lee lobbied Congress, and in 1962 he was given $40,000 to study the feasibility of bringing educational television to American Samoa.[76]

Armed with data from the study, mined by educational researchers from the University of California and Berkeley and the National Association of Educational Broadcasters, Lee in 1963 asked Congress for $3,173,740 to build thirty new schools and $2,579,000 to build a six-channel VHF tele-

Figure 2.6. Students taking a televised lesson in American Samoa.
Courtesy of pagopago.com

vision station and two state-of-the-art production studios. A wary Congress approved the school buildings, but held back $1 million of the money requested for the station until some success could be demonstrated. Lee would have to settle for only three channels at the project's onset. The broadcast station, erected atop the island's second tallest mountain, Mount Alava, became operational in 1964. A staff of 150 people imported from the mainland took the roles of principals, curricular consultants, producers, engineers, artists, photographers, and set painters.

In an era of huge cost overruns common to large government projects, the Samoan project ran only 1 percent over budget, so in 1966 Congress happily approved the additional $1 million to add the three additional channels. The studios atop Mount Alava cranked out an impressive 200 lessons per week, each running 8 to 25 minutes long, each one corresponding to the grade level it was intended to meet. The lessons ran the gamut from simple "talking heads" style of lecturing from a podium to a smaller number of field-based sessions. In general, the students received approximately eight hours of instruction by television per week, which worked out to about 30 percent of their school time (figure 2.6). After class was over, the station broadcast two to four hours of teacher training.[77]

Things began to unravel as the rigidity of the pace set from the central-ized television authority programming overran the students' ability to watch; as one teacher complained, "The TV kept coming." Teachers wanted more flexibility and autonomy, and they resented the centralized lesson planning, which resembled direct-instruction pedagogy. The central office rejected any of their attempts to contribute to the planning, so teachers often divided their classrooms into smaller sections, using bookcases to partition the room for simultaneous television viewing, discussion, and supervised practice.[78]

Rex Lee resigned his post and left American Samoa in 1967. His succes-sor was Wayne Aspinall, his lieutenant governor and the son of a powerful congressman. Lee had tried to block Aspinall's appointment as lieutenant, and there was animosity between the two men. Shortly after he took of-fice, Aspinall cut back on the hours of television instruction and began to dismantle the project by not renewing contracts with advisers such as the National Association of Educational Broadcasters. By 1974, the use of edu-cational television had slowed down to a trickle, with only 25 of the original 150 people remaining to produce programs.[79]

In the end, the adventure in American Samoa probably wasn't the "ut-ter failure" ex-governor John Haydon accused it of being in 1970,[80] but it would be hard to call it a success. Education studies on Samoa showed that people can learn from educational television more or less as well as from traditional classroom teaching, but some problems inherent in the me-dium needed to be looked at—in particular the pace that forced students to learn together at the same rate. The top-down, autocratic nature of the American Samoan experiment is typical of the way many educational technology projects are implemented. Not only was there no initial consul-tation, in terms of curricular content and pedagogy, but the Samoan teach-ers were rebuffed in their attempts to provide the project leaders feedback. And that squashed any enthusiasm they may have had for the project.

Any technological initiative is a union of three components: the tech-nology of the delivery vehicle (in this case the television), the curricular content being delivered, and the pedagogical structure used to teach that content. In the rush to introduce educational television, organizers spent too little time on the curricular content and sought no real input from the Samoan teachers in terms of pedagogy. The educational researchers Punya Mishra and Matt Koehler have introduced a popular framework describing the interaction between these three crucial factors, called technological, pedagogical, and content knowledge (TPACK).[81]

Recorded Courses

Crossing the boundary between the correspondence schools and the broadcasters, the ability to mail audio and video recordings from a distance provided a new method for delivering content remotely. Mailed recordings have advantages over broadcasts of the same lectures, in that students consume the lessons at their own pace and can easily replay portions for better understanding. A good example is the Great Courses series, which offers a catalog of expertly produced audio and video lectures from leading professors. The high production values make these programs more compelling than your typical classroom lecture shot with a single camera and delivered unedited. Recorded Courses has set a high bar for recorded lectures. Fans of the videos have included the late senator Ted Kennedy and Microsoft founder Bill Gates, who has a collection of over 60 DVDs on topics from meteorology to American literature.[82] The courses are usually organized into eight 45-minute lectures, available as video or audio-only, on CD, DVD, and now Internet download.[83]

The company was founded as the Teaching Company in 1990 by government lawyer Thomas M. Rollins, who like the American Samoan governor Rex Lee, had a personal and formative experience using video to learn. While studying at Harvard Law School, Rollins faced an important exam on an arcane area of the law in which he was not prepared, so he obtained a series of videotaped lectures by a noted expert on the topic. "I dreaded what seemed certain to be boring. I thought that few subjects could be as dull as the Federal Rules of Evidence. But I had no other way out," Rollins recalled. But the lectures turned out to be "outrageously insightful, funny, and thorough."[84]

Rollins's company has been successful at providing engaging educational content delivered via media, but it is relatively expensive and targeted primarily at adults seeking enlightenment on topics that interest them rather than education provided by more traditional educational institutions.

Lessons from Educational Film, Radio, and TV

The siren's call of using the broadcast-style media of film, radio, and television is their economy of scale. In traditional classroom teaching, adding 20–30 students means hiring an additional teacher and footing the associated costs: space, desks, books. Not only that, but the administration has little control over the content individual teachers teach and the manner in which they do it.

The lure of the broadcast media is that it potentially solves issues of cost, consistency, and quality. First, costs are moved from paying a teacher to present the material each time for a small group of students to a fixed cost to initially create the broadcast instruction, with little or no cost for additional students. Second, the administration chooses and directly controls content. Third, the teaching quality is uniform for all students. In many recent e-learning efforts, elite universities provide lectures from their star faculty members, which is one reason the courses are popular.

In contrast with live instruction, media such as film, radio, and television offer only a one-way conversation with the student. There is no real-time feedback from students so that the instructor can sense their levels of engagement and understanding. In a physical environment, even mediocre instructors teaching impersonal 300-person introductory lecture courses are able to get a sense of this response. The current-day e-learning initiatives dismiss this give-and-take and stake claim to other advantages, such as improved instructor quality, enhanced visuals, and the ability to replay content. The broadcast media of that time (pre-TiVo) did not possess all of these capabilities, and because the lessons were presented at particular times, students were forced to proceed together in lockstep, with no accommodation for faster or slower learners.

Internet-Based Media

Around the turn of the twenty-first century, the Massachusetts Institute of Technology (MIT) and other elite universities began freely posting video of classroom lectures online, along with a course syllabus, PowerPoint presentations, and class readings, for anyone to access. In response to this emerging use for their iPod products, Apple Computer provided a clearing-house for these courses with iTunes U, which made it easy for universities to reach students through the iTunes music program.

The ease with which it is possible to post videos online using sites like YouTube and Vimeo have encouraged people to begin creating short videos on just about any topic imaginable. This too represents a huge potential of a freely available supply of supplementary learning resources. Salman

Khan took full advantage of YouTube by using screencasting tools to create videos of himself teaching over a "virtual chalkboard" and is now reaching millions of K–12 students seeking help on a multitude of topics. I look more closely at his wildly successful Khan Academy in chapter 5. ·

Making videos and other educational media available on the Internet is fundamentally different from broadcasting them. Learners choose the place and time to consume a video and can pause or replay portions of the lesson if they don't understand them the first time. Internet-based media have very low startup and delivery costs when compared with broadcast media. There are no costly transmitters to construct or maintain, and bandwidth to make media available online is inexpensive or free.

YouTube is currently the dominant provider of freely available Internet video. Founded by former PayPal employees Steve Chen and Chad Hurley, while still in their mid-twenties, YouTube went live in 2005 to provide a free and easy way for people to post and watch video on the Web. By the time Google acquired it for $1.65 billion, one year later, YouTube was already immensely popular, showing over 100 million clips a day.[85]

If media are available in small enough segments, just as the correspondence course publishers provided them a century earlier, consumers can craft a custom learning experience by assembling segments, or clips, into a coherent course on a topic, often from multiple sources. The producers of the popular Technology Entertainment and Design (TED) conference, started by the irascible information architect Richard Saul Wurman, have long made the presentations delivered at the limited-attendance TED conferences freely available online. In some sense, the TED talks serve the same role as the Chautauquas did a century earlier, deftly mixing enlightenment and entertainment. The organizers recently launched an initiative called TED-Ed that makes it easy for educators to mix clips found on YouTube from the TED conference and elsewhere.[86]

The OpenCourseWare Initiative

MIT took a bold step in 2001 by making video lectures and other core academic content from almost all of its classes freely available to anyone over the Internet. MIT committed to spending up to $100 million over the course of ten years to support the OpenCourseWare (OCW) initiative, which includes not only lecture videos but also lecture notes, problem sets, simulations, PowerPoints, and exams. This spirit of sharing runs deep in

Figure 2.7. Hal Abelson.
Wikimedia Commons, courtesy Joi Ito

the university's DNA, with MIT being one of the pioneers of the open-source software movement. One of OCW's founders, Hal Abelson, said, "In the Middle Ages people built cathedrals, where the whole town would get together and make a thing that's greater than any individual person could do and the society would kind of revel in that. We don't do that as much anymore, but in a sense this is kind of like building a cathedral."[87]

Harold "Hal" Abelson (figure 2.7) was born in 1947 and grew up on a farm in New Jersey, 50 miles from New York City, where they buried "dead chickens and dead Mafiosi." Interested in math, physics, and science, he had his first introduction to computers while working at the nearby Lakehurst Naval Air Base, where he learned to program in the FORTRAN language on a teletype terminal using punched paper. Abelson later attended Princeton University when the timesharing revolution in computers was occurring and the idea of the computer as a shared and interconnected resource, a forerunner to the Internet, began to gel. He went on to MIT for a PhD in mathematics, ultimately becoming a computer science professor there.[88]

At MIT, Abelson was a gifted teacher, winning multiple teaching awards in an institution that values research over teaching, and he has a long history of innovative research in educational technology. In 1981, he directed the first implementation of the children's computer language Logo on some of the earliest Apple computers, and he was an early promoter of new ways to teach children programming concepts.[89] Abelson has long been an advocate of open access to information, having helped found groups that promoted that idea, including Creative Commons, Public Knowledge, and the Free Software Foundation.

At the apex of the dot-com technology bubble, in 1999, MIT's provost Robert Brown formed a faculty-led council, including Abelson and headed by Dick Yue, to decide how to allocate funds for future educational technology spending. The council commissioned the elite consulting group of McKinsey & Company to make some recommendations. As a leading technology institution, MIT was under pressure to react to the Internet frenzy, and it was inundated with offers from private companies to bring the university into the Internet age. Instead, it chose to take a measured and thoughtful strategy to clarify its "core beliefs."[90]

Abelson and the council proposed a commercial site called Knowledge Updates to be marketed to MIT alumni, but in 2000 the consulting group Booz Allen Hamilton, working pro bono, analyzed the business potential of marketing Knowledge Updates commercially. The consultants looked at the various institutions then marketing educational resources, such as University of Phoenix and Columbia University, and summed up the project's prospects in a three-line PowerPoint slide, saying distance education was going to be complicated, competitive, and not likely to generate revenue.

At the eleventh hour, Abelson and the council scrapped the commercial Web site in favor of a freely available one, saying, "Why don't we just give it away?"[91] This plan appealed to MIT president Charles Vest and fit well with MIT's open-source ethos; as one professor commented, "Selling content for profit, or trying in some ways to commercialize one of the core intellectual activities of the university, seemed less attractive to people at a deep level than finding ways to disseminate it as broadly as possible."[92]

Abelson's committee worked out the details, estimating the cost of implementation to be $93 million over ten years. The idea of giving the resources for free resonated with Vest, but he knew MIT could not support the full cost of a project of that magnitude. While on a trip to New York

City, he called on an old friend who headed the Mellon Foundation, William Bowen (of cost-disease theory fame). The two men met one morning at a 43rd Street restaurant, and over a Florentine omelet, Vest outlined the idea; after breakfast, Bowen told him, "Don't talk about this to any other foundations. We're going to do it."[93]

True to his word, in 2001 the Mellon and the Hewlett Foundations provided $11 million, to which MIT added an additional $1 million to fund the project for the first two years. MIT and the two foundations would split the operating costs for the next six years, after which point, MIT would solely provide the sustaining funding.[94]

There was much internal awareness about how potentially disrupting it could be to give away the school's resources. But Vest viewed the resources more as publications, rather than teaching, saying, "Our central value is people and the human experience of faculty working with students in classrooms and laboratories, and students learning from each other, and the kind of intensive environment we create in our residential university."[95]

MIT's OpenCourseWare has had a big impact in providing educational materials throughout the world, with over 2,150 courses from MIT and other institutions now freely available. The original target audience was educators, but it turned out that, as of 2011, only 9 percent of OCW users are educators, who often mix and match the resources found on OCW to create their own custom-made online courses. Over 42 percent of OCW users are self-learners who use the resources for personal enhancement, reviewing basic concepts and keeping current in their fields. In this way, these users are the modern equivalents of the correspondence school students of a century earlier.[96]

OpenCourseWare was an innovative approach for MIT to take in the face of pressures during the dot-com era's abundance of freely available Internet resources, but it would be hard to say it advanced the state of the art in distance learning very much. The free and universal admission the Internet provided made access much easier than the correspondence schools, and the ability to choose the time when to view the lectures was a big advantage over the rigid approaches of broadcast media, but the offerings remain "filmed plays" of the university's classroom lectures and resources, made broadly available.

MIT is a very competitive university, with a 10 percent acceptance rate and an average Scholastic Aptitude Test (SAT) score of 735 out of a possible

800. The school targets the rigor and pace of instruction to match its very able student body.[97] The lack of feedback to the students, a requisite of being free, makes OpenCourseWare a good resource but not necessarily an effective option for many learners with less privileged backgrounds. The e-learning universities and the correspondence schools solved this issue by throwing people at the problem, but people cost money to employ. In the next chapters, I look at how innovators tried to provide the much-needed feedback to students using technology they hoped would have greater economies of scale than one-to-one interaction

Lessons from Internet Media

The Internet is a much more capable vehicle for delivering media than its predecessors: film, radio, television, CD, and DVD. Outside of a Web-connected computer, little equipment is needed—no expensive projectors or players, no heavy film reels to lug about—and users can play and replay media on demand. It would be easy to see Internet video as just another vehicle on the historic media roadmap, but the real potential for its impact lies in its nature as a digital object, constructed of information (bits) rather than physical atoms.

As born-digital objects, digital media are all close relatives to all of the other digital information available on the computer: text, data, or images. And these media can engage in a reflexive and interactive dance with their other digital siblings. MIT Media Lab founder Nicholas Negroponte observed that "bits comingle effortlessly. They start to get mixed up and can be used and reused together or separately. The mixing of audio, video and data is called 'multimedia'; it sounds complicated, but it is nothing more than comingled bits."[98] We have begun to see hints of this potentially powerful interaction, but most of Internet media has only evolved to the "filmed plays" stage in McLuhan's progression of media self-actuation.

MIT has not been alone in trying to make its resources more accessible. Duke University took a pioneering step in 2004 and issued 1,600 free iPods to the incoming freshman class to see how they might use them in their studies. Professors posted video and audio clips for students to download and review later. Three years later, Apple Computer institutionalized the idea by working closely with Duke, Yale, MIT, Berkeley, and Stanford to make material available in a password-protected version of the iTunes Store, called iTunes U.[99]

Going beyond the Sage on the Stage

The basic methodology behind the sage on the stage model of teaching is that the teacher, someone who intimately knows the subject to be learned and is verbally adept at conveying that knowledge, stands before the students and imparts that content for them to absorb. Unfortunately, this model presents an economy-of-scale problem when we try to move it out of the classroom. Fundamentally, all of these endeavors attempt to increase the ratio of *one* instructor to a *larger number* of students, using the technology of the day: the postal service, film, radio, television, and now the Internet.

Leaving aside any philosophical arguments as to whether the lecture model, even in person, is pedagogically sound, problems arise with all of the solutions outlined before: how to meet students where they are academically, how to set the speed of instruction to match the students' required pace, and how to provide rapid and meaningful student feedback to student work and questions.

The correspondence schools addressed these problems by breaking their curriculum into small, recombinable segments that could be tailored by a student's adviser into a custom course. The schools were keenly aware of their learner's aptitudes, and they wrote their curricula to meet their students' academic abilities. By contrast, the wonderful OpenCourseWare lectures are designed around the needs of high-achieving MIT students, not the general public. Moreover, because correspondence school students returned lessons at their own rate, they controlled the pace of instruction. Finally, the correspondence courses created a factory-style infrastructure to correct student homework on a timely basis and they provided one-to-one feedback to any questions. Timely is, of course, a relative term, with the state-of-the-art delivery technology, the U.S. Postal Service, providing slower than optimal response times.

Delivering educational content using film, radio, and television had the promise of reaching potentially large audiences in a very cost-effective manner, and the research suggests it can be an effective medium for some kinds of educational content. Many of the problems in the nature of the older broadcast media can now be mediated by new technology. The recording capabilities of digital video recorders, such as TiVo, free learners from broadcast time constrictions. Lessons can be recorded and played back when it's convenient for the student, and replayed when parts are not clear. Broadcast lessons did not have any internal mechanism for providing student feedback, and they were most effective when combined with in-class discussions.

Internet delivery of educational content solves most of the access and time problems of the other delivery forms, but it still leaves the thorny problem of rapid and meaningful feedback to student work. For-profit endeavors have an easier time addressing this than free-access initiatives like OpenCourseWare, with e-learning schools such as University of Phoenix employing online professors to do the same work they would in a classroom, correcting student work and answering questions. This of course leaves the economy-of-scale issue largely unaddressed—a single instructor can respond to only so many students.

In the next chapter I look at how the designers of teaching machines attempted to move beyond using lectures to deliver information, instead providing the content instruction and student feedback by using the technology itself. The potential of successfully achieving this would be dramatically increasing the economies of scale while making the process of education more efficient for both teacher and student.

3

Step by Step

The protagonists of the previous chapter were primarily educators with missions to convey specific curricular content to their learners; they had little or no theoretical guidance on how learners learn or how teachers teach. This chapter looks at programmed instruction through the eyes of psychologists Sidney Pressey, B. F. Skinner, and Fred Keller to see how their objectivist and behaviorist perspectives shaped their efforts to build machines that teach. The principles introduced by behaviorism during this era are important because they cast a long shadow on educational technology, even to the present day. While the validity of the behaviorist doctrine is hotly debated and many of its ideas have fallen out of favor, behaviorism has had a profound impact in many areas of modern education.

The technologies described in this chapter take a different teaching method from the media-based techniques in chapter 1 and divide the content to be learned into a series of small chunks, with the goal of leading students toward understanding step by step and at their own pace. These systems added a mechanism to provide students with instantaneous critical feedback at each step, usually in response to questions, and the students advanced through the content based on correct answers. The psychologists attacked the problem of scale at the level of feedback. The more didactic approaches of film, radio, television, and Internet media were very efficient at delivering curricular content but did not offer a scalable solution for correcting student work and adapting to students' problems in understanding. The teaching machines in this chapter applied technology that could potentially scale, and they provided the feedback that their designers' theoretical frameworks suggested were critical to learning.

Sidney Pressey and His Teaching Machine

Sidney Pressey introduced one of the first of these automated teaching machines in 1927. Resembling a large mechanical adding machine, it was used initially as an automated testing tool to relieve teacher drudgery in correcting multiple-choice tests. Pressey was influenced by many of the important ideas proffered by the nascent behaviorist psychology and progressive education movements. His struggle to have his teaching machine manufactured and adopted by school systems foreshadows the subsequent innovations, overconfident rhetoric, and failures of B. F. Skinner and his colleagues decades later.

Sidney Leavitt Pressey (figure 3.1) was born in Brooklyn, New York, in 1888, where his father served as a minister in the Congregational church and his mother worked as a schoolteacher. As a child, Pressey suffered from

Figure 3.1. Sidney Pressey with his teaching machine, 1960.
Courtesy Ohio State University Photo Archive

severe bouts of asthma, so his parents moved the family, which included a younger sister, to Minnesota, where they hoped the cooler climate might help his breathing. His father broadly read progressive writings in pastoral psychology, and while Sidney had the typical minister's son habit of questioning religious belief, he was impressed with both of his parents' commitment to service, which molded his academic and professional life.[1]

Pressey received his PhD in psychology from Harvard University in 1919, under the direction of Robert Yerkes, a psychologist, primatologist, and pioneer in the field of intelligence testing and comparative psychology. At that time, psychology was housed within the Philosophy Department at Harvard. The chairman initially attempted to thwart Pressey's efforts to take a wider range of courses, such as physiology, and most importantly, classes in the recently founded School of Education. There he became exposed to the field of educational measurement, which formed the objectivist theoretical framework for his work in teaching machines and encouraged him to find "ways that schools might be made less bumbling than I found them."[2]

Yerkes arranged a research position for Pressey at Indiana University, administering IQ tests to schoolchildren in the rural Indiana countryside. Pressey was struck with the tremendous variation in their academic abilities and how they were forced to progress together at a slow, lockstep pace that did not serve all students well. Individualization became an important factor in how Pressey viewed the educational process, and he saw testing as the means to find out how to adapt instruction to meet students where they were academically.[3]

This need for individualization sparked Pressey's imagination to find a solution to the variation in student learning he faced with the schoolchildren and also set the course for his later work on teaching machines. While in Indiana, he constructed a set of simple classroom assessments that were both fast for the students to take and easy for the teachers to score. He used inexpensive "cross-out" tests, which were sets of four 6-by-9-inch cards in a folder. Each card was printed with 25 sentences to be completed with a list of possible words (for example, "I see a man on a: *dog cow horse oak cat*"), and students were asked to cross out the words that didn't belong. Pressey's tests were significantly faster and less expensive than the Stanford-Binet tests he had been tasked to administer, yet they correlated well with them. During his four years at Indiana, he published over 53 articles and was offered a job as an assistant professor at Ohio State University in 1922, rapidly rising to the rank of full professor in 1926 and staying there for the whole of his academic career.[4]

Pressey likely was aware of the work of psychologist and philosopher John Dewey in progressive education surrounding the role of individualization in education. Dewey's student-centered approach was a visceral reaction to factory-model schools of the post–Civil War era, and he advocated for a system where students learned by experimentation, using their imaginations to develop individualized solutions to problems and learning in a social environment.[5]

In 1873, in cooperation with the University of Iowa, Dewey founded the Laboratory Schools to explore some of his ideas. In 1894, he reached out to William Rainey Harper, president of the University of Chicago and former director of instruction at the New York Chautauqua under John Heyl Vincent,[6] and he joined the Chicago faculty to establish the pioneering University of Chicago Laboratory Schools. Dewey's appointment was formative for him because he was tapped to head the department of philosophy, which combined philosophy, psychology, and pedagogy, presenting him with an interesting disciplinary mix through which to explore education.[7]

Dewey's Laboratory Schools were a hotbed of innovation that introduced some important ideas in education that Pressey embraced in developing his teaching machine. Pressey saw the factory model of schools as a threat to the individualism that he and Dewey both viewed as critical. He described education as a "tremendous mass problem. To state there must be both mass education and individualization seems to present an impossible dilemma." He pressed for methods to optimize the development of individualization and to encourage self-instruction, predicting, "There will be many labor-saving schemes, and even machines—not at all for the mechanization of education, but for freeing the teacher and pupil from educational drudgery and incompetence."[8] Pressey saw educational testing as a way to provide the technology that could return that focus back to the individual and provide a more academically nurturing role for teachers, rather than functioning simply as test administrators.

Pressey's Automatic Teacher

The earliest patent for a mechanical educational device was filed in 1809 to help teach reading, but the earliest direct predecessor to Pressey's device was patented in 1866 by carpet-making-machinery inventor Halcyon

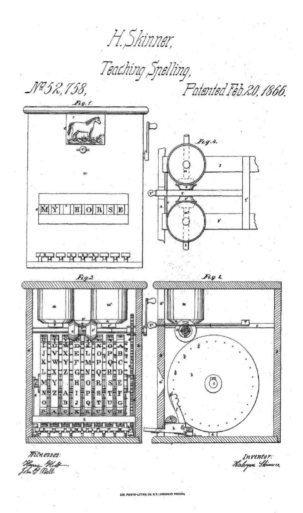

Figure 3.2. Drawing from Halcyon Skinner's patent application for an "Apparatus to Teach Spelling" (1866).
U.S. Patent Office, patent no. 52,758

Skinner (no relation to B. F.) to help students with their spelling.[9] Skinner's machine (figure 3.2) worked by presenting a series of pictures with eight rotatable wheels underneath containing letters the spellers could manipulate to spell out the picture. Historian of psychology Ludy Benjamin argues that Halcyon's device does not qualify as a true teaching machine because it had no mechanism to provide direct feedback to students as to the correctness of their responses.[10]

Sidney Pressey wanted to improve education in much the same way that the physicians and physical scientists around him were doing for their respective fields. This "discipline envy" was the result of observing the rich array of technological innovations flourishing during this period, such as radio, refrigeration, aspirin, and vaccines. His fellow psychologists evidently must have felt the same pull because by 1930, one-quarter of the 25,472 psychological research articles were educational studies, and of the 700 patents issued on educational technology by the U.S. Patent Office between 1890 and 1930, half of them were issued in the 1920s alone.[11]

Pressey saw educational testing as the technology he wanted to leverage to bring the scientific method so successful in the hard sciences into education. The psychology writer Edward Boring believed that Pressey may have had the idea for his teaching machine as far back as 1915, while he was still a doctoral student at Harvard, but it wasn't until 1921, after the interruption of World War I, that he first published reports about it.[12]

Pressey introduced his machine on December 29, 1924, at the annual meeting of the American Psychological Association in Washington, DC; with 267 members in attendance, it was the largest turnout in the association's history.[13] (Today, over 12,000 people attend the event annually.)[14] Pressey showed a nicely crafted machine assembled from $50 worth of old typewriter parts and "functioning as an automatic intelligence testing machine," rather than the teaching machine it eventually would become (figure 3.3). A series of multiple-choice questions were wrapped around the old typewriter's platen, exposing only one question at a time, arranged in order of difficulty. The subject would respond by pressing one of the four keys presented, and the platen would rotate to expose the next question when a correct answer was pressed.[15]

Pressey filed his first patent for the device in 1926, with the title "Machine for Intelligence Tests"[16] exactly a year after the APA meeting, but the evolution in his mind from testing machines to teaching machines was already under way. That same year, he published a paper titled "A Simple Apparatus which Gives Tests and Scores—and Teaches," outlining how the same basic mechanism could be employed to "teach informational and drill material more efficiently, in certain respects, than the 'human machine.'" As dismissive as that might have sounded, Pressey saw his device as a way

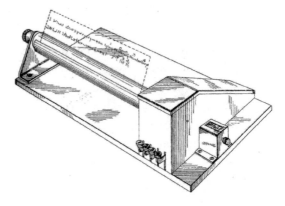

Figure 3.3. Detail from Sidney Pressey's patent application for an intelligence testing machine (1926).
U.S. Patent Office, patent no. 1,670,480

to free the teacher from drudgery, likening his teaching machine to the adding machine, which had liberated bank clerks from the tedium and inaccuracies of manual addition; thus, the device would "leave the teacher more free for her most important work, for developing in her pupils fine enthusiasms, clear thinking and high ideals."[17] This theme occurs frequently in justifying educational technology initiatives, from educational radio to the more recent flipping of the classroom* ideas promoted by the Khan Academy and others.

The redesigned device had some new features that promoted learning over testing, such as a mechanism that could keep students on the same question until they answered it correctly and a counter that recorded how many times the student answered correctly. Pressey also added a dispenser that provided a small piece of candy when the student answered a certain number of questions correctly.[18] A researcher later joked that he could identify the brighter students in the classroom by the stickiness of their little fingers.[19]

Like many of the psychologists of his time, Pressey was a "closet behaviorist" and did not self-identify as one in public. He felt the current ortho-

---

*Flipping the classroom is a technique by which students learn the curricular material themselves, often using videos, and the teacher uses precious classroom time to work with students individually.

Figure 3.4. Edward L. Thorndike, around 1912.
Published in *Popular Science Monthly* 80

doxy of introspection* did not have enough rigor to provide much insight into the problems found in education, as compared with the emergent behaviorist movement, with their strict reliance on the scientific method.[20] Contrary to what many people currently believe, behaviorism did not originate with Skinner but had its roots decades earlier in the work of psychologists John Watson and E. L. Thorndike, who had a particularly strong theoretical influence on Pressey.

Edward Lee Thorndike (figure 3.4) was born in 1874 in Williamsburg, Massachusetts, yet another son of a minister, from a family that dated its

---

Introspection relied on self-observation to gain insights into the mechanisms of thought, rather than empirical or experimental evidence.

arrival in America back to 1630. He attended Harvard University, hoping to study under William James, but instead began conducting psychological research using children. When he had trouble finding human subjects, he switched from children to chickens, convinced that animals could provide insight into human learning.[21] Harvard unfortunately would not let him keep the chickens on campus for some reason, and therefore he had to conduct the experiments from the basement of William James's home, supposedly using books as maze walls.[22] (This fate did not befall Skinner's use of pigeons in his experiments decades later.) Thorndike transferred to Columbia University to complete his PhD in 1898, and he stayed there until his death in 1949.

Thorndike was uncannily prescient on how technology might automate learning, saying in 1912, "If, by a miracle of mechanical ingenuity, a book could be so arranged that only to him who had done what was directed on page one would page two become visible, and so on, much that now requires personal instruction could be managed by print."[23]

Thorndike originated many of the key concepts that define behaviorism as we now know it, including the S-R (stimulus-response) connection and the principles that strongly influenced Pressey's design of his teaching machine. Thorndike's *law of effect*, later called *reinforcement theory* by Skinner, posits that if learners receive a satisfactory result for an action, it tends to strengthen their connection with a situation, whereas an unsatisfactory result tends to weaken the connection. Pressey's design actualized this principle, rewarding students by advancing them forward only if they gave correct responses.

Thorndike's *law of recency* stated that the item most recently learned will be the one most remembered, and this is evidenced in Pressey's machine because the last answer chosen by the student is always the correct response. Finally, Thorndike's *law of exercise* said that the things most repeated will be the ones best remembered and was embodied in Pressey's teaching machine, which required students to answer two correct answers in a row in order to properly modulate the amount of practice needed.[24]

Pressey was driven to commercialize his teaching machine, which he dubbed the Automatic Teacher. This may have been due to the earlier success he had selling the cross-out test booklets he had developed in Indiana. Classroom testing had become routine during the 1920s, so Pressey and his wife were able to sell hundreds of thousands of booklets printed with twenty separate tests and over 2 million blank booklets.[25]

Between 1925 and 1929, he contacted over a dozen American companies to manufacture the Automatic Teacher, but each effort was met with rejection. A. C. Watson, the president of the Marietta Apparatus Company, an Ohio company that manufactured psychological experimentation equipment, passed on the opportunity but gave him some constructive criticism. Watson's feedback had a lasting influence on Pressey, who realized that "my problem is financial, not scientific,"[26] and that a commercial product needed to be inexpensive, adaptable to multiple situations, and require little preparation to use.

Pressey's big break came in 1929, after three years and a dozen rejections, when he signed a contract to manufacture the Automatic Teacher with M. W. Welch Manufacturing, a respected, family-owned manufacturer of scientific instruments based in Chicago. Impatient after years of pitching his idea, and heeding the advice he received from A. C. Watson, Pressey offered to forgo any royalties on the first 200 units sold if Welch priced the machines at $5 per unit, and he later offered to personally pay for the $1,200 tooling costs required for manufacture. Welch knew how long schools took to adopt a new technology, and he took Pressey up on his offer to pay the tooling costs but graciously gave him a 100 percent royalty on the $15 selling price he needed until the $1,200 was recouped.[27]

Welch began to advertise the Automatic Teacher in May 1929, and he authorized $3,000 to allow the tooling process to begin. Pressey worked closely with Welch to fine-tune his design into a manufacturable product. He barraged the company with demands for refinements, causing the tooling costs to rise to over $5,000. This meant that Welch would lose a significant amount of money on the first hundred units made and needed to sell more than 250 machines just to break even. Thus began a long battle between Pressey and Welch over the workability of Pressey's design and the quality of Welch's manufacturing. There were endless alignment and stability issues that caused teachers many problems using the device in the classroom.[28]

In the end, the failure to heed A. C. Watson's advice doomed the Automatic Teacher to sell only 127 units, well below the threshold to break even financially. The $15 price was too expensive for schools to afford, being more than half of the $29.27 annual per-pupil education cost at the time.

Also the machine was inflexible, unreliable, and difficult to implement, which caused tension and a lack of adoption by schools. In 1930, as the effects of the Great Depression deepened, and sales to schools looked even bleaker, Welch discontinued the sale of the Automatic Teacher with 160 unsold units in stock.[29]

The stress in manufacturing the Automatic Teacher took a toll on Pressey's marriage and his health. The company that had successfully published millions of the novel test booklets he had devised in Indiana closed as a consequence of the growing depression, and his wife and partner in the failed venture divorced him for another man, which left him with strong feelings of abandonment even four decades later. Ever resilient, Pressey married a fellow Ohio State faculty member (and his ex-wife's best friend) in short order. He stopped working on teaching machines for the next decade, developing a simple punchboard testing device for the U.S. Navy during World War II.[30]

In the end, Pressey blamed the failure of his teaching machine on the Great Depression, which made it "ironic to facilitate the progress of young people into careers where no careers could be found or save labor in teaching when there were many more teachers than jobs." He also blamed the reluctance of schools to adopt new technology, lamenting, "Education is the one major activity in this country which is still in a crude handicraft stage."[31] The feeling was echoed by Skinner in 1958 as he pitched his own version of a teaching machine: "Pressey's machines succumbed in part to cultural inertia; the world of education was not ready for them," yet he also criticized Pressey's psychological theory, saying it "had not come to grips with the learning process."[32]

Interest in teaching machines lay dormant until Skinner's work in the 1950s, but Pressey made a significant contribution to the then nascent world of automated testing. In recognition for his work at the intersection of psychology and education, Pressey was honored in 1962 with the first prestigious E. L. Thorndike Award for "distinguished psychological contributions to education" from the American Psychological Association, which, among other things, formally recognized him as the "grandfather of the teaching machine movement."[33]

B. F. Skinner and His Teaching Machine

B. F. Skinner's entry into the world of teaching machines came as a result of unbridled enthusiasm from his successful experiments in modifying animal behavior. He proposed a new way to explain learning through *operant conditioning*. The concepts of shaping and reinforcing behavior by rapid and continuous feedback have set the theoretical foundation in automated instruction for over a half a century. Initially unaware of Pressey's work, Skinner began by testing crude mechanical devices where students took many small steps towards understanding by being asked to respond at each step and provided rapid reinforcement for correct answers. Pressey and Skinner would spar for decades over the basic constructs and implementation details of their respective approaches to automated instruction.

Burrhus Frederic Skinner (figure 3.5) was born in 1904 in Susquehanna, Pennsylvania, an idyllic town on the winding Susquehanna River. His father was not a minister but a small-town lawyer, who passed the bar examination just as Thomas Jefferson and Abraham Lincoln did, by reading law under the guidance of a local lawyer. Fred, as he was called, was named for his mother, Grace Madge Burrhus, who, according to Skinner, was "rated as a beautiful woman" and was the dominant force in the Skinner household, which was increased to four by the birth of a second boy two years later. Both boys were interested in science and mechanical toys such as Erector sets, chemistry sets, and models of working steam engines, which no doubt fed Fred's future interests in tinkering and invention.[34]

During high school, Skinner worked for a struggling shoe store in Susquehanna that had adopted the speculative practice of Practipedics, or the "science of giving foot comfort" that "knows feet as well as shoes" by providing a variety of support inserts for shoes.[35] Following the model pioneered by the International Correspondence Schools, the Graduate American School of Practipedics offered a correspondence course that Skinner passed to become a practicing practipedist but his personal foray into small business was less than successful.[36]

Skinner's father, William, had a flourishing local law practice and harbored political aspirations, but these were dashed when he successfully defended a strikebreaker in a murder trial, which caused him to lose political support in the union-dominated town of Susquehanna.[37] When business began to wane, William moved the family to Scranton, Pennsylvania, in 1920, to take a position as assistant general counsel to the Hudson Coal company, hoping, in vain, to succeed his boss over time.[38]

The young Skinner attended Hamilton College, in upstate New York, in 1922, where he joined a fraternity and studied biology, the humanities, and

Figure 3.5. B. F. Skinner and his wife, Yvonne (Eve), around 1936.
Courtesy Julie Vargas

writing, ultimately majoring in English literature. It would be a chance encounter with the famous poet Robert Frost that cemented his desire to
become a writer. During his junior year Skinner stumbled into Frost when
he went to an empty lecture hall to play the piano and heard his fellow students in an adjoining room cry, "Stop playing! Robert Frost is reading his

poems!" Frost and Skinner had lunch that day, and upon learning of the younger man's interest in becoming a writer, Frost encouraged him to send him some of his work.[39]

Like many parents of students who proposed professions with lower odds of success, Skinner's parents were less than pleased when he wrote them during his senior year about his plans to become a professional writer. His father responded with a lengthy and thoughtful letter hoping to dissuade him from that path, writing, "Appreciation of art, music, and literature is a great asset for college professors, librarians, and teachers generally, but it will not put any 'butter on your bread.'"[40]

Skinner was torn as to his future direction, but on April 7, 1926, he received a letter from Frost in response to the poems and essays he had sent him a year earlier. After apologizing for the delay in responding, the great poet wrote that he saw promise in Skinner's writing: "I ought to say that you have the touch of art. The work is clean run. You are worth twice anyone else I have seen this year." This finalized Skinner's decision to return to Scranton after graduation and commit a year to writing, insisting to his parents he be allowed to "try my wings."[41]

The fledgling author became discouraged with writing as a career after failing to write anything substantive, complaining that "nothing in my history has led me to take a position on any important issue." He began reading books by psychologists such as John Watson, E. L. Thorndike, and Ivan Pavlov and became fascinated with their behaviorist perspectives. He posed the following desert island question to himself, pitting the writer George Bernard Shaw ('A') against the psychologist Ivan Pavlov ('B') and asking, "If 'A' is drowning on one side of a pier and 'B' is equally drowning on the other, and you only have one life belt and cannot otherwise help, to which of the two would you throw it?" Skinner chose Pavlov and applied, and was accepted, to Harvard's graduate school for the fall of 1928 to study psychology.[42]

Skinner maintained his passion for writing throughout his life and was a prolific author. Over the course of his life, he published more than 16 books, including the novel *Walden II*, three lengthy autobiographies, three works on behaviorism aimed at the general public, and several highly influential academic volumes.

Harvard proved to be a stimulating environment for Skinner, and a hotbed for the nascent behaviorist movement emerging in psychology, but he spent his time split between psychological and physiological work involving nervous system reflexes. He was mentored by the renowned physiologist William Crozier and was mainly left alone to pursue his own research interests; the psychology department assumed the physiology department was supervising him, and the physiologists assumed the psychologists were directing him. As a result of the mutual neglect, he had plenty of freedom to explore, to his great benefit.

Because researchers at the time tended to make their own equipment, the Harvard psychology department operated an extensive machine shop to construct experimental apparatus. The machinist who ran the shop had recently died and was "replaced only by a framed photograph," so the graduate students had full run of the shop and its extensive supply of mechanical parts.[43] This autonomy proved invaluable to the mechanical skills he would need in his later research efforts. Skinner made good use of the opportunity and ultimately invented several tools, including the cumulative recorder, which recorded experimental results on long rolls of paper. The recorder allowed him to analyze a stream of events over time and to graphically visualize the data to gain insights.[44]

There was much camaraderie and discussion among the Harvard psychology graduate students, but one student was the most influential for Skinner by far. His friendship with Frederick Simmons Keller (figure 3.6) would last six decades and spawned a scientific correspondence that rivaled that of Thomas Jefferson and John Adams. The two lived in the same apartment complex in Cambridge, often walked to the university together discussing issues in psychology, and helped each other with their laboratory experiments. Keller was instrumental in convincing Skinner to embrace behaviorism, and he would be an important contributor in applying programmed instruction into the classroom.

Skinner's study of psychology was highly empirical. He resented the way even venerated psychologists applied human motives to their animal subjects, saying things like "he likes that" or "he holds his attention too long." In his opinion, the psychologist who voiced these kinds of thoughts was as traitorous to his science as "the astronomer who comments on a beautiful sunset, knowing full well that the sun does not 'set.'"[45] This insistence on observed evidence helped him establish a more scientific tradition for psychology.

His insistence on using data to guide his thoughts permeated his personal life as well. In 1931, Skinner began noticing his hair thinning out,

Figure 3.6. Fred Skinner, Fred Keller, and Charles Ferster at Skinner's Festschrift dinner, 1970.
Courtesy of the B. F. Skinner Foundation

presumably as a result of inhaling mercury fumes from a rat experiment he was running. He searched the literature and found that the chemical hexlyresorcinol might restore his hair, and he constructed an experiment to test the hypothesis. Each morning he carefully counted the last hair strands and plotted the numbers on a graph; the data led him to the sad conclusion that the chemical had no effect on his hair loss, which did not end until he stopped using the mercury in his experiments.[46]

Skinner received his PhD in 1931 and spent the next five years doing research on operant conditioning, after which he took a teaching position at the University of Minnesota. Just before leaving Cambridge, he met Yvonne (Eve) Blue, who had studied English at the University of Chicago and had taken several courses from the author Thornton Wilder. After a six-week courtship, he and Eve were engaged and moved to Minneapolis.

The Heir Conditioner

Any story about B. F. Skinner would be incomplete without a discussion of his infamous baby tenders. The baby tender was essentially a baby crib where a child could stay during the first year of his or her life. Instead of having vertical bars, the baby tender was an enclosed climate-controlled box with a glass front. It was also the reason for Skinner ultimately becoming one the best known psychologists in America, and perhaps the most controversial—a fame that would inhibit the adoption of his teaching machines a decade later.

Skinner and Eve Blue married in 1936 and had their first daughter, Julie, in 1938. Eve apparently did not to like some of the chores associated with early childhood, so when she was pregnant in 1945 with their second daughter, Deborah, Skinner set out to use technology to ease her issues. He constructed the device to replace the crib, bassinet, and playpen. Debbie could sleep in the baby tender atop a stretched canvas on rollers and in a heated environment (this was Minnesota, after all) without the need of constricting blankets.[47]

The Skinners were pleased with Debbie's first nine months in the baby tender, noting she was healthy and happy, and the box did indeed prove to be a labor-saving device for Eve. Skinner began to explore marketing the device and approached General Mills, which had funded part of his earlier Project Pigeon experiment, to manufacture it under the clever moniker the Heir Conditioner. He also publicized it in an article he titled "Baby Care Can Be Modernized," written for a popular woman's magazine of the day, the *Ladies Home Journal*. After much internal debate at the magazine, and insistence that a pediatrician examine Debbie, the magazine published the piece in 1945, using the provocative title "Baby in a Box."[48]

A firestorm of controversy ensued about the cruelty of using the device and the lack of personal contact it engendered. The tenders were in fact used like traditional cribs, and children placed in them (myself included) received the same amount of contact from parents as did any other child reared behind bars. Skinner's older daughter wrote that "to the end of his life Skinner was plagued by rumors about his second daughter, hearing even that she had committed suicide. In fact, Skinner was an affectionate father and never experimented on either of his children. Deborah is a successful artist and lives in London with her husband."[49]

Skinner unsuccessfully tried to market the baby tenders over the years and was discouraged from patenting the device because it was considered obvious* in the eyes of the law and therefore unpatentable. This early frustration clearly lessened his resolve to pursue manufacturing of his teaching machines a decade later. He did however, draw up plans to distribute among his colleagues, including Lloyd Homme, Ben Wyckoff, and Jim Gray, who manufactured baby tenders in small quantities for eager adherents to the behavioral religion (such as my parents). Jim Gray commented that "even if just the nuts buy them, there is a sizeable market."[50]

Skinner's experience with the heir conditioner helped him develop a national reputation as an innovator and a maverick, and it only bolstered his willingness to put controversial ideas to the general public. These skills would serve him well as he later promoted his ideas on radical behaviorism and education using teaching machines.

Project Pigeon

It's not clear whether Harvard's decision to allow pigeons on campus stemmed from the school's being impressed with the results Thorndike achieved from his chickens or simply the fact that they were not barnyard animals. Regardless, the pigeon ultimately became Skinner's animal of choice for his experiments. He had an early appreciation for the bird, formed during a visit he made as a child to a country fair where a troupe of performing pigeons cleverly acted out a scene of firemen saving a pigeon family from a three-story house fire.[51] Although his early work involved laboratory rats, he later preferred pigeons as experiment subjects because they were more active in their environment, which allowed him to make faster discoveries about their reactions to changes.

To encourage the pigeon's curiosity, Skinner would withhold their feeding to reduce them to 80 percent of their normal weight so they were more motivated to peck for food rewards. My mother used to sing to me a little ditty that the 1950s Harvard behaviorists used to chant to the tune of the Roto-Rooter ad jingle: "Starve your pigeon, to eighty percent. They'll perform, like any lady or gent."[52]

---

*U.S. patent law does not permit the patenting of ideas considered obvious to "one skilled in the art," such as trying to patent the wheel.

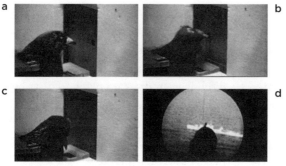

Figure 3.7. Frames
from a World War II
film demonstrating
Project Pigeon.
U.S. Navy

While at the University of Minnesota during World War II, Skinner embarked on what he later called a "crackpot idea, born on the wrong side of the fence intellectually, but eventually vindicated in a sort of middle-class respectability." His plan was to use trained pigeons to guide armed missiles toward their targets. Some may have had some issues with the ethics involved in putting innocent animals at the center of certain death, but he justified it, viewing their sacrifice as small relative to the devastation Hitler's relentless bombing was causing in Europe. Radar had not yet been invented, and the complex servomechanical equipment of the day required to guide a missile would have left little room for explosives.[53]

Skinner began the training process by the showing the pigeon a dot projected on a translucent screen and, using the technique called shaping, would reward the bird with food when it pecked on the dot (figure 3.7a–c). *Shaping*, or successive approximation, is a process Skinner developed to encourage specific behaviors he wanted by rewarding small steps toward that action.[54] In the beginning, any motion a pigeon made toward the screen would be rewarded; as it consistently acted in the general direction of the desired behavior, the criteria would grow more and more specific until the bird was doing exactly what Skinner wanted. He later moved the dot back and forth and the pigeon would follow quickly and precisely track the dot, ultimately training it to track a battleship (figure 3.7d). In essence, Skinner was using the bird as an animal computer, performing a complicated tracking operation that the technology of the day could only crudely perform but which, over the course of millions of years, evolution had equipped animals to do perfectly. There is a wonderful short video of this on the B. F. Skinner Foundation's Web site.[55]

While he was teaching at the University of Minnesota, the U.S. Navy gave Skinner a small grant of $25,000 to pursue project ORCON (for ORganic CONtrol). His group constructed a set of optical lenses at the tip of the missile's nosecone, which focused the missile's forward view onto a screen placed in front of each of the three pigeons strapped inside. A pneumatic mechanism then steered the missile toward its target based on a mechanical "vote" of two out of three birds agreeing on the direction.

Project Pigeon worked beautifully in a number of tests for the Navy, but it was abandoned partly in favor of more promising research efforts, such as the Manhattan Project, and because the idea of pigeons guiding a bomb was a difficult sell to the academic review panels and the military brass. Almost two decades later, Skinner lamented, "a pigeon was more easily controlled than a scientist serving on a committee," adding, "There is a genetic connection between teaching machines and Project Pigeon. We had been forced to consider the mass education of pigeons."[56]

Skinner left the University of Minnesota in 1945 to head the psychology department at Indiana University. Two years later, during the fall of 1947, he was asked to deliver the prestigious William James Lectures on psychology at Harvard. While in Cambridge, he was wooed back to Harvard by his old mentor Garry Boring, who offered him a full professorship and extensive funding to equip and staff his laboratory; he remained at Harvard for the rest of his academic career.[57]

Skinner's Teaching Machine

Skinner took a great interest in his children's education but rarely interfered in their schooling, outside of once complaining about the two hours of homework his daughter Julie had to do each night, saying that her schooling amounted to a "something over a forty-hour week. I cannot believe that the work of ninth grade requires that much time." While attending a father's day back-to-school event at his youngest daughter Debbie's school on November 11, 1953, he watched with the other fathers from the back of the class as her teacher taught fourth-grade arithmetic. After writing the problem on the blackboard, the teacher would walk up and down the aisle, occasionally pointing out the children's mistakes. Some students finished quickly and sat bored while others continued to work the problems. The papers were collected, graded by the teacher, and returned to the students the following day.[58]

This immediately gave Skinner insight into some problems in the pedagogy, as well as an idea toward their solution. The lockstep pacing forced students to progress together regardless of their individual abilities and without immediate feedback to their actions. Skinner knew that a corrected paper seen 24 hours later could not serve as a reinforcer and did not present a good scenario for learning. Understanding the value of using mechanical devices in his work with pigeons, he created a crude prototype over the next few days, using a series of cards containing questions, within a box with sliders to "dial in" the answers (figure 3.8). It was his first teaching machine.[59]

The following year, the University of Pittsburgh asked Skinner to talk about some of the practical applications of his work in behavioral science, and he presented a paper entitled "The Science of Learning and the Art of Teaching." After talking about training pigeons to play ping-pong, he turned his attention to education. He described classroom education as a set of stimuli and responses between the student and teacher, estimating there were probably 25,000–50,000 such interactions during the first four years of school. He went on to describe an inexpensive machine he had designed to accomplish it:

> A small box about the size of a record player. On the top surface is a window in which a question or problem printed on a paper tape may be seen. The child answers the question by moving one or more sliders upon which the digits o

Figure 3.8. One of Skinner's first teaching machines.

through 9 are printed. The answer appears in square holes punched in the paper where the questions were printed. When the answer has been set, the child turns a knob . . . If the answer is correct, the knob turns freely and can be made to ring a bell or provide some other conditioned reinforcement. If the answer is wrong, the knob will not turn. The knob can then be reversed slightly, and a second attempt at a right answer made.[60]

Skinner was probably truly unaware of Sidney Pressey's earlier attempts at introducing the teaching machine, as they were a full generation earlier and Pressey had stopped actively working on them in 1932. When Pressey learned about Skinner's new device from a 1954 article in the *Science News-Letter*, he sent Skinner a letter, quipping, "when I saw your pigeon demonstrations at the Cleveland meeting last year I wondered if something of this sort might be in the offing. I shall expect to see a busy child in a similar display case in New York this September," and he enclosed reprints of his earlier papers on his efforts in teaching machines.[61]

Whatever tension the letter had caused, it was dispelled when Pressey and his second wife had breakfast with Skinner at the 1954 meeting of the American Psychological Association in New York City, where they had a positive and exciting discussion that seemed to contradict Pressey's pessimism and discouragement from two decades earlier. Although it took him four years, Skinner acknowledged Pressey's previous work in his 1958 paper on teaching machines in the prestigious journal *Science*, and he continued to acknowledge his predecessor publicly from that point on.[62]

Skinner may have had a little bit of guidance from the court of public opinion in acknowledging Pressey. A popular "gossip" column in the journal *Contemporary Psychology* reported, "[Lloyd] Homme, by the way, has been at Harvard for the past year, working on another idea that originated with Skinner, the technique for teaching by machine."[63] Horace B. English, a colleague of Pressey's at Ohio State (and a witness in the landmark 1958 *Brown v. Board of Education* trial) alerted the column's author, Edward Boring (a Harvard colleague and former professor of Skinner's), to Pressey's earlier work on teaching machines; Boring asked Skinner who he thought had invented the teaching machine. Skinner wasn't sure the real inventor could be identified, pointing to Halcyon Skinner's 1866 teaching machine as one contender, but he did say that Pressey was certainly the first psychologist to take the matter seriously.[64]

Programmed Learning

Sidney Pressey had used E. L. Thorndike's laws of effect, recency, and exercise to explain the theoretical basis for using his teaching machine to possibly improve student learning. Skinner's machine also may have been influenced by Thorndike's law of effect, which says that when a response is followed by a satisfying state of affairs the strength of their connection is increased, but he eschewed mentalism, or the sense of self, that Thorndike attached to learners being "satisfied." Skinner focused only on observable responses that he could empirically record, and he proposed a new theory of how people learned, which he called *operant conditioning*. It was this emphasis on observable behavior that gave him confidence that his experiments on laboratory animals would lend insight into how people learned, and his view was "teaching is a matter of arranging contingencies of reinforcement under which students learn."[65]

Believing that learning occurs when desired behaviors are systematically reinforced, Skinner theorized that learning could be accomplished by *programming*, where the student is led in a directed manner through the content by taking many small steps, each step requiring a response. The student receives immediate feedback for that response and moves forward to the next step only if his answer is correct. In this way, the student controls the pace of learning and only moves forward only when the content is fully mastered.[66]

Skinner proposed that programming would take the role of the teacher by designing a series of questions in the manner a teacher might teach, through a series of small approximations toward the goal, not unlike his training of the pigeons in his World War II missile heads. This idea of *dialectic teaching*, or leading a student using a series of directed questions was presaged in ancient Greece. In Plato's *Meno*,[67] the philosopher Socrates leads his friend Meno's uneducated slave boy successfully through solving geometry's Pythagorean theorem by asking him to respond to a series of small questions that direct him toward the solution. A researcher in 1962 cleverly programmed a lesson for a teaching machine based on the *Meno*, by adapting Plato's words to walk a modern student toward solving the same geometric problem.[68]

Skinner designed his steps, which he called *frames*, to be as small and as directed as Socrates's questions to Meno's slave boy. Each frame built on what the student already knew and expanded on that knowledge toward the next frame. While the steps are small, a skillful programmer could create a gradual progression where the steps were chained together to create more complex understandings over time.[69] Skinner's goal was to minimize the percentage of wrong answers to under 10 percent so that he shaped the learning from one response to the next. If students made too many errors, the steps were considered too large and the program was revised.[70]

Russian psychologist Lev Vygotsky in the 1930s described this idea of building slowly on what the learner already knows and extending out from there in his concept of a *zone of proximal development* (ZPD). Vygotsky's theory can be visualized as a series of enclosed circles: the outermost circle contains the material to be learned, the innermost circle contains the material the student already knows, and between the two circles is the content the student can learn with some guidance (figure 3.9). Vygotsky believed that the most efficient place for learning occurred in this middle area, the zone of proximal development.[71]

Skinner's idea of a series of small steps, designed in a gradual progression toward a learning goal, was very much in line with Vygotsky's concept of the ZPD. Skinner designed his frames to draw on what students already knew; he then ventured just outside these to introduce new concepts that would ultimately be integrated into the innermost circle of student knowledge.

It was important to both Pressey and Skinner that their teaching machines help a student thoroughly understand the content being taught in a particular session before moving on to the next. An average grade would not do. Known as *mastery learning*, this idea allowed them to trade time for ability and have students set their own pace of learning. Students with less ability took more time to master the material and were not frustrated with moving too fast or publically embarrassed by their slower pace. Students with more capacity advanced more quickly through the content and were not held back at a pace that bored them. But all students attained the same level of mastery.

The idea of mastery learning was first popularized in the 1920s by Henry Morrison, a disciple of John Dewey at his innovative University of Chicago Laboratory Schools, and it left a lasting impression on American classroom education. Besides mastery learning, Morrison introduced the

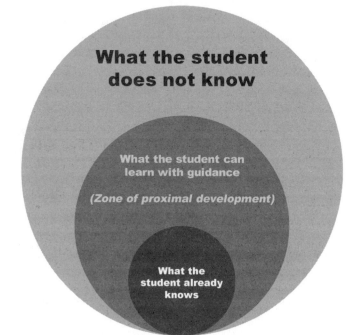

**What the student
does not know**

What the student can
learn with guidance

(Zone of proximal development)

What the
student already
knows

Figure 3.9. Lev Vygotsky's Zone of Proximal Development.

modern concept of dividing the curriculum into units (science, language arts, etc.), making a conscious distinction between the content itself and how it was being taught, and the systematic instructional cycle of *pretest, teach, test the result of instruction, change the instruction, reteach,* and *retest.*

Henry Clinton Morrison was born in 1871 and worked as a pioneering public school superintendent throughout New England before joining the University of Chicago Laboratory Schools in 1919.[72] He saw mastery as significant change in the personality of the student and contrasted it with the status quo: "In lesson-learning, the teacher said, 'this pupil has worked seven of every ten lessons correctly and receives a grade of 70.' In mastery, the teacher says 'this pupil has definitely caught the central idea.' He exhibits in his daily work the concepts he has mastered. Bookishness has been converted to true learning."[73]

Making Skinner's Teaching Machine

Skinner did not seem to have the same entrepreneurial urges that Sidney Pressey evidently had, but he understood that for teaching machines to be used in schools, somebody needed to manufacture them. He engaged the Harvard administration to seek a solution, and they identified a wealthy alumnus, Sherman Fairchild, who had given millions to fund a biochemistry laboratory and was on the board of IBM and had some contact with IBM's upper management. In September 1955, IBM approached Skinner with the traditional first step of sending a nondisclosure agreement. "I saw no reason why I should sign it," he said, "but was told I would have to do so, unless I intended to file a patent application," which he promptly did, in May of the following year.[74] In the meantime, Skinner worked out an oral agreement with IBM executive Gordon Williamson in November for IBM to investigate for manufacturing the physical devices; he also arranged for patent rights and established a foundation to support the development of programming for the new machines.[75]

Not used to the slower pace of manufacturing, Skinner was frustrated with the lack of progress. IBM assigned the construction to their venerable electric typewriter division and, true to its internal culture, the company decided to use punch cards to hold the questions. Ten trial machines were slated to be built for testing in a school the following year, with sale to the general public to begin in 1958. However, IBM terminated the agreement and left Skinner with only a plaster model of the machine the company was supposed to build.[76]

Skinner's original design used multiple dials containing numbers or letters, which the student spun to answer the questions, so it was suitable only for simple arithmetic and spelling applications. Interested in branching out to other subject areas, such has chemistry and physics, he worked out a new design. With the help of a $25,000 grant from the Ford Foundation in 1956, Skinner asked the Harvard machine shop to build a version that used a large paper disk on which 30 questions rotated through a small slit (figure 3.10). Students wrote their handwritten responses on a strip of paper that scrolled through another slit. When the student finished, he or she would pull a lever, the strip would scroll to hide the handwritten response, and the disk would rotate to reveal the correct answer. These new devices were used by Harvard students in a popular class on natural sciences taught by Skinner's colleague James Holland.[77]

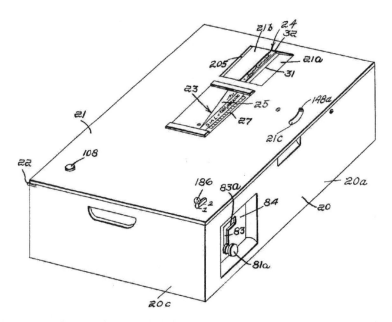

Figure 3.10. Detail of B. F. Skinner's second-generation teaching machine.
U.S. Patent Office, patent no. 2,987,828

Skinner tried a second time to find someone to manufacture his teaching machines, and he signed a deal with a California-based steel drum manufacturer, Rheem, in 1958, based on the new model that supported handwritten answers. He had wanted to call the device the Auto-Didak, but the name was shortened to Didak because of the pejorative sense of the original word referring to a self-taught person. Like IBM, Rheem would ultimately disappoint Skinner; the two parted company in 1962, and Skinner continued to look for a company to realize his idea using wood, plastic, or metal.[78]

Partly out of this frustration, and as if to answer E. L. Thorndike's 1912 wish for a book that dynamically presented its pages to the learner,[79] Skinner and Holland created a teaching machine in which the mechanical apparatus of levers and dials were replaced by pages in a printed book. *The Analysis of Behavior* was a complete course in the principles of behavior analysis in 337 pages. Every page was divided into six parts vertically, with each part containing a "track" of questions. The student would answer the question within it, such as "In the knee jerk reflex, the kick of the leg is the _____to the tap on the knee," and then turn the page to see the correct answer.[80]

The public had met Pressey's teaching machine with indifference, but the reaction to Skinner's ranged from a sense of wonder and excitement to fear and anger about the mechanization of schools and the dehumanization of the student-teacher relationship. A flurry of articles ran in the popular magazines, including "Will Robots Teach Your Children?" in *Popular Mechanics* and "Can People Be Taught like Pigeons?" in *Fortune*.[81] But it was Sidney Pressey who had the most nuanced and critical reactions to Skinner's "invention," and he wrote several articles describing them.

As similar as the mechanics behind the two men's teaching machines were, Pressey and Skinner had fundamental differences as to how they were to be used and what theoretical basis explained their learning results. Pressey saw his machine more as an adjunct to traditional instruction or simple reading, being used to support fluency and practice. Skinner viewed his solution as the primary source of instruction and saw the programming as the most important component of the teaching machine, saying, "The machine itself, of course, does not teach. It simply brings the student in contact with the person who composed the material it presents," and that material was delivered by the program.[82]

Pressey objected to the minute steps into which Skinner's programmed instruction broke the content, particularly when compared with simple reading of a textbook. He did an informal study in 1964, looking at the actions required to work through Holland and Skinner's programmed book. Pressey found that the average student could read the written textbook section in 10 minutes; by contrast, the same content in the programmed book took 41 minutes to complete because of the time needed to execute the requisite 84 responses and their accompanying page turns. Students received essentially the same score using either technique when tested on the material (19.51 vs. 20.08).[83] Pressey's claim that *The Analysis of Behavior* was slow and tedious anecdotally agrees with the opinions of many of the psychologists I interviewed for this book.

Skinner felt it was important for students to compose their own answers rather than selecting from a number of possible choices in which only one was correct. He likened the difference to having a reading knowledge of a foreign language as opposed to having the ability to speak in that tongue. He also didn't like the fact that three out of four possible answers were wrong, saying wrong answers were like static and interfered with the reception of ideas. Pressey argued that allowing wrong responses could potentially show up misconceptions in the students' cognitive processes (e.g., adding one versus subtracting one).[84]

In response to this debate, researchers performed several studies in the 1960s to test the efficacy of the different approaches. Three independent research teams compared writing the answers in Skinner's method to choosing from a set of multiple-choice answers, as Pressey advocated. Two of the researchers found no significant difference between the two techniques, and the third found only modest gains for the constructed answer method.[85]

The behaviorist Thomas F. Gilbert, a former colleague of Skinner's (and my mother's second husband), advised educators against using teaching machines in a 1960 *Fortune Magazine* article, using his customary provocative manner: "If you don't have a gadget called a 'teaching machine' don't get one. Don't buy one; don't borrow one; don't steal one. If you have such a gadget, get rid of it . . . The so-called teaching machine is a disease."[86] He would also add, "If you want to buy a machine, get a toaster."[87]

Sputnik and the American Classroom

On October 4, 1957, at the height of the cold war, the United States received a wakeup call from the Soviet Union. The launch of a satellite the size of a beach ball into a low-earth orbit ignited a fear that America was losing its technological dominance. The 184-pound Sputnik (Russian for "fellow traveler") was visible to the naked eye as it orbited the earth every 96 minutes (figure 3.11). "Words do not easily convey the American reaction to the Soviet satellite," Roger Launius, the former chief historian of NASA wrote. "The only appropriate characterization that begins to capture the mood . . . involves the use of the word hysteria."[88] That hysteria would reverberate over the American psyche, the military industrial complex, and the nation's public education system.

Fanning the flames of fear was the former assistant director of the Manhattan Project and "father" of the U.S. Navy's atomic submarine fleet, Admiral Hyman George Rickover. Rickover viewed Sputnik's launch as a triumph of Russian education and saw the United States lagging behind in

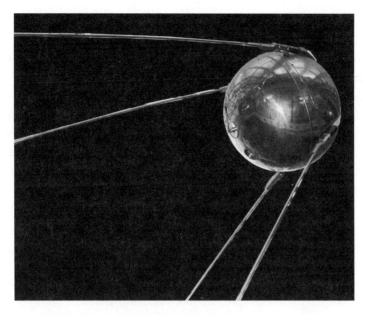

Figure 3.11. Model of the Sputnik I satellite.
NSSDC/COSPAR 1957-001B, National Space Science Data Center/NASA

producing the scientists and engineers he deemed necessary to compete with the Soviets. "Education is the most important problem facing the United States today," he wrote, "and only the massive upgrading of the scholastic standards of our schools will guarantee the future prosperity and freedom of the Republic." His call for a better educated populace prompted a national outcry for a more effective and rigorous school system in America and, not surprisingly, advocated technology as a means toward this end.[89]

Every generation seems to have its own Sputnik incident, some story that creates a crisis of faith in the effectiveness of American education. The Flexner report, published in 1910, ushered in a wholesale modernization in the way American doctors were trained.[90] In 1946, President Harry S. Truman's Commission on Higher Education concluded that American education levels "are still substantially below what is necessary," and the publication of *A Nation at Risk* in 1983 criticized the state of American schools and spurred the computerization of the American classroom for the following two decades.[91]

In response to Sputnik, the United States swiftly launched a series of private and public initiatives to catch up with the USSR, including the

National Aeronautics and Space Act of 1958, which created NASA, and, more important to the story of teaching machines, the National Defense Education Act (NDEA), which funded educational initiatives to train the scientists Americans would need to compete in the new space race with the Soviets. The NDEA provided hundreds of millions of dollars through grants to promote research and experimentation on, among other things, audiovisual "aids for presenting academic subject matter through such media," as well as direct funding for schools to purchase audiovisual equipment.[92] This new funding was often matched by grants from private foundations such as the Ford and Carnegie foundations.

The large influx of money fueled the development of educational television and many high-profile classroom trials of teaching machines. Concerned over the shortage of qualified teachers at the time, and high on Sputnik fever and readily available funding, several psychologists (who probably should have stayed in their laboratories) created 1960s versions of the modern high-tech start-up, foreshadowing the later forays by computer scientists into the educational business world.

The Commercialization of Teaching Machines

Even though Skinner may have cooled to the idea of manufacturing teaching machines himself, his colleagues eagerly took up the cause in much the same way they had done for his baby tender. By 1962, there were over 73 commercially available teaching machines of various shapes, sizes, and theoretical persuasions.[93] Skinner disciples Ben Wyckoff and Lloyd Homme hopped on the bandwagon to form Teaching Machines Incorporated (TMI), which became one the largest manufacturers of teaching machines in the country, and Allen Calvin's Behavioral Research Laboratories conducted several high-profile experiments using teaching machines in K–12 schools before launching his own venture.

L. Benjamin Wyckoff was a reluctant academic who studied under Skinner at Indiana University in 1947. He was quickly drawn into Skinner's worldview of behaviorism, including a strong belief in its ability to make a difference in society. Wyckoff and Skinner shared common research interests, and both enjoyed building experimental apparatus, so Skinner asked him to work with him at Harvard during the summer of 1950 on some experiments involving pigeons and color perception. At the end of that summer, Skinner invited him to finish his studies at Harvard, but Wyckoff

Figure 3.12. Full-page ad for TMI-Grolier Min/Max teaching machine (1961).
Milwaukee Journal, Mar. 29, 1961

demurred and returned to Indiana to finish his PhD because he did not want Skinner's dominant personality to interfere with his personal research agenda.[94]

Wyckoff did not seem to like the ever-present stress of university politics and administrative duties at the schools where he taught, which included the University of Wisconsin and Emory University. In 1959, he left academia for good to join a company with some old classmates from Indiana, Lloyd Homme and Robert Glaser, also Skinner acolytes. They founded Teaching Machines Incorporated to manufacture the teaching machines that Skinner was not able to do. TMI manufactured a series of inexpensive ($20–25) devices, called the Min/Max (for minimum time/maximum learning). The Min/Max was essentially a better-engineered version of Skinner's second-generation teaching machine using standard-sized, 8-1/2-by-11-inch sheets of paper.[95]

While other teaching machine companies focused primarily on the hardware, TMI approached the problem from the "software" side of the equation, the programming. TMI developed many programs for the Min/Max, covering English, basic and advanced mathematics, science, several foreign languages, and music. Their broad solution attracted a distribution agreement with the encyclopedia publisher Grolier in 1960, which advertised to a wide audience (figure 3.12) and used a sales force consisting of 70 ex-school superintendents.[96] Grolier eventually sold over 150,000 teaching machines before TMI went out of business in 1965.[97]

Teaching Machines in the Classroom

The late 1950s and early 1960s saw a severe shortage of qualified classroom teachers, which was further exacerbated by the large influx of new students from the post–World War II baby boom.[98] The fear induced by the Sputnik launch prompted massive investments in education by the government, private foundations, and publishers and created a perfect combination of circumstances for a series of highly publicized experimental trials of programmed instruction initiated in public schools across the country. Multiyear trials in the Roanoke, Virginia; Gary, Indiana; Newton, Massachusetts; and Manhasset, New York, school systems provide some clues into the complex issues of introducing instructional technology into schools.

Heeding Sputnik's call, Allen Calvin, a young psychologist at Hollins College, in Roanoke, Virginia, had been intrigued with Skinner's earlier work in teaching machines. In 1960, with the blessing of Hollins's president John Everett, he applied for a grant from the Carnegie Foundation to study their use in the classroom.[99] Calvin received $68,000 over three years to test programmed instruction with the college's undergraduate and graduate language students. He and the head of the Hollins language department, Maurice Sullivan, planned to use the machines to teach linguistics, vocabulary, and grammar. But a preliminary experiment to teach algebra in a Roanoke city high school stunned the researchers with the students' rapid progress through the material.[100]

Calvin worked closely with the superintendent of the Roanoke Public Schools, Edward Rushton, to test teaching machines with students in February 1960. Rushton methodically gained the cooperation of the school board, the principal, the teachers, and the parents at a middle school for the trial. He selected 34 eighth-grade students who were *not* slated to take classroom algebra the following year to take a programmed instruction course in algebra. They used mechanical teaching machines, manufactured by equipment-maker Foringer and using programmed instruction developed by a Hollins graduate student (a high-school math teacher).[101]

The results were very encouraging. Using just the programmed instruction and no teacher intervention, the students were able to complete the yearlong algebra course in just one semester. When tested using the same assessments used for the ninth-grade students, the eighth graders achieved the average grades of the older students taught by the traditional methods. Calvin tested the group a year later and found an astonishing 90 percent retention rate, encouraging him to expand the trial to more students and subjects, presumably with the blessing of the Carnegie Foundation.[102]

In September of the next year, they broadened the experiment to three Roanoke high schools, involving more than 900 students and 11 teachers in 32 classes in algebra I, algebra II, and plane geometry (figure 3.13). Rather than use mechanical teaching machines, they wrote a programmed textbook similar to the Holland-Skinner book for instruction. The students were randomly assigned to one of three experimental groups. In the *control* class, students were taught conventionally using a teacher and a textbook. In the second group, called the *help* class, students were taught using programmed instruction books, but the teacher was free to help the students in any way they requested. The third group, the *no-help* class, also

Figure 3.13. Students at work during the Roanoke, Virginia, programmed instruction experiment.
Courtesy of Encyclopaedia Britannica

learned through the programmed books, but the teacher could not directly help them.[103]

Neither the help nor the no-help class was allowed to do homework, which of course delighted the students but worried some of the parents, who asked, "Why is there no homework? Why is my child in a class without a teacher?" and the perennial bane of academic researchers, "Why is my child being used as a 'guinea pig' in an experiment?" As it turned out, most students using the programmed instruction finished their year's work by December. The difference between the help and no-help conditions was small in general, with better results for the students who received no help from the teacher.[104]

The experiment vindicated many of the key precepts in Skinner's theories regarding programmed instruction. The face-saving advantage of individualized pacing was evident in one student's comment, "The eggheads don't get slowed up; the clods don't get showed up." Another student reflected on the value of immediate feedback by saying, "I like the idea of knowing if an answer is right without having to work a lot of examples and then find out the next day I've done them all wrong." Addressing the concept of learning through shaping or successive approximation guiding to a proper response, another student said, "I like the way it's given in small easy to understand statements and not one big chunk."[105]

The success of the project attracted the attention the publisher of the venerable *Encyclopaedia Britannica*. Encyclopedia publishers were important sources of information after World War I, amassing large and effective sales teams to sell their expensive volumes. It is no wonder why the nascent market for teaching machines presented an irresistible sales opportunity, targeting both K–20 students and adult learners. Just as Ben Wyckoff had made an alliance with the Grolier Encyclopedia, Calvin struck a deal with Encyclopaedia Britannica Films (EBF), in May 1960, to develop programmed mathematics books and machines under the brand TEMAC (for TEaching MAChines). Calvin would devote his attention to the project full time and employ a staff of six Harvard, MIT, and Indiana doctoral students to develop the curriculum for EBF.[106]

Encyclopaedia Britannica was encouraged by the work being done at Hollins and looked to expand the production by proposing an institute to be headed by Calvin, called the Center for Learning and Motivational Research. It was to be housed at Hollins College, but Hollins trustees turned down the request.[107] On September 1, 1961, Allen Calvin personally piloted his family in a private Cessna airplane to Palo Alto, where the institute was established on the Stanford University campus.[108] The institute thrived for several years before EBF closed it in 1968, amid allegations of financial improprieties and charges of mismanagement.* Warren Everote, EBF's president, said that though the company had great drive, "It is a drive, however, that is best attuned to setting up a conspiracy for a second-rate revolution in a third-rate country rather than managing a first-rate educational program."[109]

Nevertheless, the Roanoke experiment continued to influence EBF. There was a revolving door between the publishers, the academics, and the school administrators involved in automated instruction, which is eerily reminiscent of the flow of public officials in Washington between government and industry. In the end, all of the leading figures from Roanoke would be employed by EBF, including Hollins president John Everett, Roanoke schools superintendent Rushton, and the three Hollins professors who worked on the project.

*Allen Calvin told me, on August 3, 2013, that the reason for closing the center was because "EBF was primarily interested in the direct production of programmed textbooks which would make money for them" rather than conducting basic research in programmed instruction he and his staff wanted to perform. He sued EBF and reached a settlement that enabled him and Sullivan to start Behavioral Research Laboratories.

Calvin went on to found Behavioral Research Laboratories (BRL) in 1963, with his fellow Hollins refugee Maurice Sullivan, and successfully produced programmed instruction material. In 1970, after Calvin had left the company, BRL took over the complete instruction for a failing elementary school in Gary, Indiana. In a no-contest bid arrangement, the company received $800 per pupil to take full control of the Banneker School using its programmed instructional texts, provided it was successful in raising the student test scores.[110] While preliminary test results were encouraging, BRL was ejected from the school because of intense litigation from teachers and their unions.[111]

Fred Keller's Personalized System of Instruction

It became increasingly clear to researchers that success in using programmed instruction did not lay in the apparatus but in the design of the instructional materials. Skinner's friend Fred Keller and his colleagues molded operant conditioning constructs into a more effective system of instruction that could be easily delivered on paper without requiring physical machines. Even Skinner himself had abandoned the use of machines after he and Jim Holland wrote the programmed-instruction book *The Analysis of Behavior.*

It is ironic that Fred Keller, who was a much more jocular and extroverted personality than Fred Skinner in person, tended to stay out of the spotlight of the general public. Keller was a psychologist's psychologist. While at Columbia, he and Skinner kept up a steady correspondence, debating and refining issues of learning and reinforcement theory, and he fed Skinner a steady stream of post-doctoral psychologists (including my father) for his laboratory over the years.

In 1961, Keller became interested in seeing how the new learning theories might be used for college instruction and accepted a Fulbright-Hays* invitation to teach reinforcement theory at the University of São Paulo. He became entranced with Brazil while the Brazilian psychologists became entranced with his ideas. In 1964, he returned to the University of Brasilia, in the newly created capital city deep within the Amazon. While there, he de-

---

*Fulbright-Hays is a U.S. Department of Education program that provides grants for overseas projects for teachers, students, and faculty engaged in a common endeavor.

veloped a system to use programmed instruction in the classroom, informally called the Keller plan, or personalized system of instruction (PSI).[112]

PSI followed all the precepts found in programmed instruction—self-pacing, mastery learning, rapid feedback—and applied them to a live classroom situation. The plan consisted of dividing the semesters content material into 25 or so units, arranged in a logical progression. Programmed instruction material and other resources would guide students through the unit, and they were tested by proctors selected from students in the previous semester. Students could move on to the next unit only if they fully mastered the content. They could discuss the material, and even debate the proctor on wrong understandings, but only an A-level performance would be accepted. Finally, students worked at their own pace.[113]

Linear and Branching Approaches to Programmed Instruction

Two distinct schools of thought emerged among the proponents of programmed instruction. Skinner, Keller, and their disciples strongly believed in a more *linear* and *constructivist* approach to the programming, in which students followed one path through the material and generated the answer, as opposed to choosing from a list of multiple options. Skinner hated the idea of the multiple-choice format because it necessarily contained wrong answers that students might remember. Because he was progressively shaping learning toward a specific goal, Skinner and his colleagues advocated for a linear ordering of the information en route to that goal.

In contrast, the *branching* approach, promoted by former U.S. Air Force psychologist Norman Crowder, embraced the wrong answers students chose. Crowder saw these incorrect responses as an opportunity to provide remedial instruction by routing students to different places in the instruction based on what kind of wrong answer they gave. He viewed this adaptive branching as a superior method to teach more complex and nuanced problem-solving skills, such as teaching topics like labor-management relations. Crowder used both teaching machines and a popular collection of scrambled books, published by Doubleday, which had readers dart back and forth through the text based on their answers.[114]

Crowder viewed Skinner's behavior model of human learning as naive and felt it did not really describe how people learn. He disdained using any formal theory, saying that a programmer "is no more committed to any specific theory of learning than is the writer of any other type of expository text." Crowder did not divide his content into such small steps as the linear programmers did, relying instead on larger chunks of material. He believed this made the learning quicker than with linear approaches, where the students had to go through the instruction from beginning to end, regardless of their prior knowledge.[115]

Crowder introduced the notion that the program could *adapt* to what the student already knew and should offer material that met their current understanding. Like a good tutor, the program would present appropriate remedial material to guide students to understanding things they did not yet know based on their incorrect answers. This adaptive ability would prove to be an important component in later artificial-intelligence-based approaches to automated instruction. In fact, Crowder's work might have had a better chance of success in the age of the personal computer. The electromechanical devices he relied on were expensive and cumbersome to program, and while the scrambled books were cheap to distribute, they were equally expensive and cumbersome to program and awkward for learners to use.

Making Sense of the World of Programmed Instruction

One of the most important methodologies behaviorists brought to modern psychology was the rigor of the scientific method of experimentation. That empiricism spurred objective studies on teaching machines and programmed learning. The results of those studies were mixed, with automated instruction typically faring as well as or better than conventional teaching in terms of learning objectives and knowledge retention over time. Where they *did* outshine traditional classroom instruction was in the time it took to accomplish that learning, being typically 50–100 percent faster.

Why Didn't Programmed Instruction Succeed?

In spite of experimental evidence suggesting they were effective, schools failed to adopt teaching machines and programmed instruction in any large measure. Was this because of basic issues in their theoretical constructs? An issue of expense? Was the technology of the time not up to the task? Was there too much pushback from the status quo?

The objectivist and behaviorist theoretical backbones that Pressey and Skinner relied on were well suited to the devices they built, but it's not clear that they represented the best pedagogical technique to teach all kinds of content material. In fact, they worked best only in very specific areas such as mathematics. Additionally, the idea of slowly shaping a student toward an answer has led many people to question whether the broader context of the topic can be understood by using such small steps.

The philosopher John Searle proposed a clever scenario that raises this question: Can a learner actually know a topic by properly responding to only small requests? His Chinese Room thought experiment proposes that an English-speaking person is locked in a room with a book containing instructions in English on how to respond to questions in Chinese (figure 3.14). People place questions written in Chinese under the door, and the person inside the room follows the book's instructions on how to turn the questions into well-formed answers written in Chinese. The question Searle asks is, does the person actually understand Chinese?[116]

The timing of the Great Depression clearly undermined Sidney Pressey's attempts to get schools to use his teaching machine. By the 1950s and 1960s the economy had regained its strength, but costs to produce quality programmed instruction unfortunately had grown quite high, typically more than $175,000 (over $1 million in today's dollars), and it took over 15,000 man-hours from highly skilled authors to create a typical linear programmed instruction course. Branching programs required even more time and money to accommodate the many extra branching frames needed to react to different answers.[117]

There was a lot of pushback from schools, teachers, and the public, to adopting programmed instruction in the classroom. The ubiquity of public schools makes them an attractive target for purveyors of instructional technology, who see a large potential market for their products but often fail to understand that budget-constrained school systems have little room for discretionary spending.

With the notable exception of Allen Calvin's Roanoke project, teaching machine advocates made no attempt was made to garner "buy-in" from those tasked to manage the classroom, the teachers. As many times as Pressey and Skinner claimed that these tools would free teachers from tedium and allow them to be better guides for their students, teachers nonetheless felt their primacy in the classroom was threatened, and they actively resisted the new devices. The perception was that teaching machines were in fact taking control of the curriculum away from them and effectively "teacher-proofing" instruction.

Figure 3.14. Chinese room thought experiment.
Courtesy Daniel Dennett and Neil Cohn, visuallanguagelab.com

Finally, the notion of individual pacing has remained antithetical to the industrial-era factory model of a graded classroom system, which has been the model of schools for the past century. Schools are just not equipped to deal with students who do not learn in age-progressed groups, even if this system is clearly one that consistently fails its students. Fred Keller's personalized system of instruction gained limited acceptance in postsecondary education but was never adopted in K–12 schools.

Programmed Instruction's "Big Ideas"

In spite of the various shortcomings in the design and implementation of programmed-instruction teaching machines, they offered four promising ideas:

1. *Individual pacing* is perhaps the most important issue separating programmed instruction from traditional classroom instruction, and the only attribute it shares with the more didactic methods of the correspondence course and videos on demand. Pressey, Skinner, Keller, and Crowder all made removing lockstep pacing from instruction a critical component of their systems. Whether the steps they substituted were big or small, they allowed students to move at their own rate and ability.
2. Henry Clinton Morrison's concept of *mastery learning* was a critical requirement for successful learning. Getting a C or even a B would not do; only full mastery of the content would allow the student to progress to the next unit of information. Coupled with individual pacing, mastery allowed students to trade time for ability and previous content knowledge, and it removed some of the embarrassing situations less able students often felt with traditional classroom instruction.
3. Learners received *rapid feedback* to their answers, as opposed to waiting a day or more for a teacher to correct their work (or even weeks in the case of mail-based correspondence school courses). Rapid feedback provided a motivating experience for the student, and it kept their focus on moving forward instead of wallowing in misconceptions.
4. Norman Crowder's flavor of *adaptivity* in his branching programmed instruction courses presaged later artificial-intelligence-based approaches that modified instruction based on student responses and promised to have the instruction meet students where they were academically, showing respect for their time.

B. F. Skinner admitted in 1989, "Computers are now much better teaching machines,"[118] and they do indeed perform better than electro-mechanical devices and scrambled books. Programming becomes the dominant component in the overall teaching machine and makes possible a richer set of interactions with the student than can be accomplished solely from metal and plastic.

The next chapter looks at how the following generation of teaching machines tried to harness that potential reflexivity and add the adaptivity that mechanical devices and scrambled books could only hint at. It was now the computer scientists' turn to take the reins of teaching machines from the psychologists. Their solutions relied more on the emerging digital computer and networking developments and less on ideological learning constructs.

4

Byte by Byte

The next generation of teaching machine innovators put aside the mechanical toys of their youth and embraced the new universal machine of their day, the digital computer. Like the behaviorists in the preceding chapter, these engineers and computer scientists believed they had found the secret to teaching within the capabilities of these new devices, but for the most part, they did not rely on psychological theories of learning to guide them.

From the very start, the computer was indeed different. In the mid-nineteenth century, Charles Babbage conceptualized the first mechanical computers, which he called the Analytical Engine and the Difference Engine. The massive Difference Engine (figure 4.1) resembled a large organ grinder's instrument, with a series of gears that could be manipulated to "crank-out" solutions to numerical equations. The eccentric Londoner was fortunate to count among his friends Ada Lovelace, the precocious daughter of the poet Lord Byron. Lady Lovelace suggested that instead of using gears to specify the calculations to perform, he might use punched paper cards, like those that controlled the complex patterns in fabric mills, saying, "the Analytic Engine weaves algebraic patterns just as the Jacquard-loom weaves flowers and trees." Unfortunately, Babbage never completed building his mechanical beast, but the concept of a generalized and programmable computing machine entered the zeitgeist and was refined over the next century by Alan Turing, Jon von Neumann, and a host of others.[1]

In spite of their massive physical size, huge price tags, and limited capabilities, the first modern computers were fundamentally identical to the personal computers that permeate our lives today. They could take a mass

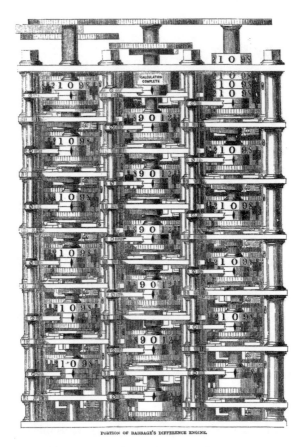

PORTION OF BABBAGE'S DIFFERENCE ENGINE.

Figure 4.1. Drawing of a portion of Babbage's Difference Engine (1864).
Harper's Magazine 30, no. 174 (1864): 3

of information, present it to a user according to a set of rules, allow the user to respond in some manner, and then present some other information based on that response and according to another set of rules. This infinite programmability and capacity to provide a custom-tailored response made the computer an ideal candidate for the next generation of teaching machines, and the idea of computer-aided instruction (CAI) was born.

The first successful use of a computer in education was the Programmed Logic for Automated Teaching Operations (PLATO) system, begun in 1960 at the University of Illinois, which introduced a more interactive and conversational relationship between the "instructor" and the student. While never commercially successful, PLATO was developed for over five decades. It was a pioneer in e-learning, and it contributed many innovations to computer-aided instruction and computing in general, including online forums, touch screens, and plasma displays.

With the advent of the more affordable and accessible personal computer in the 1980s, Seymour Papert, a mathematician and computer scientist at the Massachusetts Institute of Technology, was intrigued by how these machines might teach in a wholly different manner from either the didactic classroom lecture or the rigidly structured approaches of the behaviorists. Strongly influenced by the ideas of the Swiss psychologist Jean Piaget on constructivist learning, Papert believed that the open-ended and exploratory nature of the personal computer could be used in education in a more meaningful manner.

The growing ubiquity of the personal computer made truly interactive applications available on inexpensive and increasingly powerful home devices, but without being tethered to costly mainframe computer systems. The seemingly unlimited space found on CD-ROMs offered an opportunity to deliver rich multimedia experiences previously impossible, and volumes of "edutainment" disks quickly became de rigueur for middle-class parents and their children.

Finally, like the behaviorists before them, artificial intelligence researchers were convinced that they too were onto breakthroughs about how to teach by using machines. The 1990s brought a flurry of activity in developing "intelligent tools," called intelligent tutoring systems (ITS), to tutor students by "understanding" what they already knew and instructing them on what they still needed to learn.

PLATO

Compared to the teaching machines previously discussed, PLATO represented a new philosophical approach. The Chautauqua, correspondence schools, radio, and television were driven by educators, or at least by business people trying to sell education. The mechanical teaching machines and programmed instructional tools were ideologically motivated by their objectivist and behaviorist theories of how people learned and could be taught. The PLATO project was driven by engineers, and engineering has a methodology much different from that of the previous two disciplines. Engineers tend to see large problems as a collection of smaller problems that

Figure 4.2. PLATO founder Don Bitzer.
Courtesy Don Bitzer

in turn need to be solved, and this reductionist approach was most evident in PLATO's design.

Donald L. Bitzer was a 1950s engineer straight out of central casting, both in looks, with his crew cut styled haircut, and in his Apollo 13 "make it happen" attitude. Bitzer (figure 4.2) was born in 1934 and always knew he wanted to be an engineer. He pored over issues of *Popular Science* magazine and built radios and other electronics before attending the University of Illinois for his bachelors, masters, and doctoral degrees in electrical engineering. He worked as a researcher at Illinois before joining the faculty, where he taught for the bulk of his career. After retiring from Illinois in 1989, he moved to North Carolina State University, where he became Distinguished University Research Professor in the Department of Computer Science.[2]

As with the other educational technology innovations of the day, educational television and mechanical teaching machines, the 1957 Sputnik launch provided a strong impetus for the University of Illinois to create technological tools to improve education. The inability of the United States to create a workable rocket was a huge embarrassment to the Illinois engineers, who jokingly dubbed the effort with the nickname "civil service," "because it wouldn't work and they couldn't fire it."[3]

In 1959, Bitzer was just 26 years old and working as a lab assistant at the university and listening to heated discussion of a faculty committee meeting across the hall. At the School of Engineering, researchers were trying to make the transition from defense work to peacetime research efforts and had identified education as a possible future direction to explore. Dan Alpert, the dean of engineering, had formed a committee to investigate computerized learning systems, but the group was unable to find an appropriate solution. Alpert was about to throw in the towel and admit failure. But knowing that Bitzer had also been thinking about computerized education, Albert asked his opinion about what to do. True to his engineering persona, Bitzer replied, "Give me a week, and I'll let you know."[4]

Like any classically trained engineer, Bitzer attacked the problem systematically and thought about the components that would be needed. He identified the most critical components to be a display flexible enough to present a wide variety of image, text, and graphical elements and a more dynamic way for learners to interact with the machine. The state of the art in communicating with a computer was the teletype, which was essentially an electric typewriter. You would type something, and the computer would respond after a few seconds by typing something back. There were no real graphics, images, or charts, and the process was painfully slow. Bitzer remarked "it was hard enough to teach, without putting up with being handicapped by the restrictions on the media you had to use."[5]

Early PLATO

To create the first PLATO system, Bitzer used a 1950s vintage ILLIAC (for ILLinois Automatic Computer) left over from the lab's early defense work. But the capabilities of early computers were extremely limiting. The ILLIAC used 2,800 vacuum tubes, weighed over 5 tons, had only 64,000 bytes of memory, cost over $1 million to build in today's dollars, and could perform 1,300 calculations per second.[6] (To get some perspective on this, my Macintosh Air weighs about 2 pounds, has 8 billion bytes of memory, costs around $1,000, and can do an astounding 30 million calculations per second.)

What Bitzer was able to coax out from ILLIAC's limitations was truly amazing. PLATO 1 looked much like any modern CAI system, albeit a little cruder and slower. Instead of a teletype, Bitzer used a television that could display interactive text and graphics and a 16-button keyboard that displayed directly on the screen (figure 4.3). Lessons were stored as frames (up to 64) in an "electronic book" that could be combined with video generated by the computer onto the "electronic blackboard." The hardware was largely built using existing parts, and the cost to make the first generation of the PLATO terminal was just under $5,000.[7]

Students used PLATO by reading the information on the screen. When a response was required, they typed it on the keyboard, and the answer appeared instantly on the screen. If the answer was correct, the system passed the student to the next screen in the lesson; if it was wrong, the system presented a remedial question on the material. At any point, students could press the HELP key, and the problem would be sub-divided into

Figure 4.3. An early PLATO terminal.
Courtesy Don Bitzer

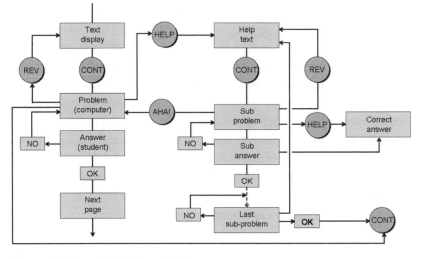

Figure 4.4. How PLATO-1 worked.
Adapted from D. Bitzer, P. Braunfeld, and W. Lichtenberger, "PLATO: An Automatic Teaching Device," *IRE Transactions on Education* 4, no. 4 (1961): 159–60

a series of smaller steps. When they finally understood the material, they could hit the AHA! key and progress to the next frame (figure 4.4).

The PLATO system had no real educational or psychological theory as a foundation. Bitzer was clearly aware of earlier teaching machine efforts, and even though the initial pedagogical methodology was kill and drill, using M&M candy as reinforcement, the team took great pains to distance PLATO from Skinner's theories. Over time, they added more sophisticated teaching techniques, such as graphical and algorithmic simulations, to the simple drill practice. The system also had the potential for increasing critical-thinking skills through its open-ended answer approach, which used clever answer-judging software to analyze student responses and could discriminate between a misspelled word and a truly wrong answer.[8]

The PLATO system had many of the positive features common to earlier teaching machine efforts: students moved through the course at their own pace. They had to master a section before moving on to the next. They received immediate feedback to their responses, which were constructed rather than chosen from multiple-choice answers. Finally, a hint of adaptivity that helped tailor the teaching to students' individual understanding was available in the elaborate help system provided.[9]

The TUTOR Language

In the beginning, course lessons were programmed using a computer language tailored to the specific computer, requiring someone skilled in the arcane coding of mainframe computers. This made the creation of course content slow and expensive to produce, something on the order of $400–800 per instructional hour.[10] In 1967, a zoology graduate student, Paul Tenczar, wrote a simple, English-like language to program PLATO content, called TUTOR.[11] TUTOR could describe powerful pedagogical scenarios but was simple enough for nonprogrammers to understand and even enabled teachers to program their own lessons without working through a programmer as an intermediary, so that Bitzer could say, "The fruit fly lesson was written by a biologist, the geometry lesson by a mathematician, and the lesson on organic chemistry by a chemist."[12]

TUTOR made it possible for teachers to easily write sophisticated lessons using charts and graphics, as well as program full simulations that instantly reacted to student responses, for example, showing the effects of joining atoms into molecules. Tenczar's answer-judging software made it possible to differentiate student responses, allowing PLATO to tell the difference between wrong answers and simply misspelled responses. The judging capabilities also made it possible to shape answers, in very much the same way Skinner's operant conditioning techniques nudged students toward understanding. Answer judging made that nudging more targeted toward areas where the student had trouble, which provided a some degree of adaptivity to the lessons.[13]

PLATO-IV

Even though the TUTOR language dramatically lowered the cost of creating courseware, the overall costs of using the system were still too high for successful commercialization to the schools. The price tag to deliver an hour of instruction was between $2 and $5, which at the time was not even competitive with human tutors. Bitzer knew he needed to lower the costs to less than 35 cents per hour for schools to be able to adopt PLATO, and this meant more innovation. He and his colleagues applied to the National Science Foundation (NSF) and received $4.5 million in funding between 1968 and 1972 to redesign PLATO so it might scale.[14]

The first versions could support only three students at a time and tied up a huge mainframe computer in the process. The PLATO team needed to support more users, and they developed a way to connect the terminals via phone lines rather than expensive video lines, eventually supporting over 1,000 students simultaneously. They invented a gas plasma display that supported touch technology like a modern iPad, so students could tap on the screen to respond, and they lowered the terminal's cost from $5,000 to under $2,000.[15]

This ability to connect students with one another also had some positive unintended consequences: it fostered a community of learning and led to the formation of the first online learning forums. These new advancements sparked a long chain of innovation, both directly, by inspiring the creation of the Lotus Notes collaboration application (now part of IBM), and indirectly, by influencing researchers at Xerox's Palo Alto Research Center (PARC) and, through PARC, the development of the Apple Macintosh.[16]

Was PLATO Successful?

PLATO was designed to augment classroom instruction, typically for only an hour per day, and by all accounts, it was an effective tutor. The NSF funded a $1 million evaluation of PLATO in 1978, conducted by the Educational Testing Service (ETS), and while it fared well on ratings of student effect, ETS summarized, "In light of the overall evaluation, it can be concluded that PLATO had no significant impact on student achievement in this implementation and demonstration."[17]

This result is not unusual in the world of educational research when two methods of teaching are compared with one another. A long-running debate between the educators Richard Clark and Robert Kozma has questioned the value of doing these kinds of media studies, which often end up showing no significant difference between methods. Clark used the following analogy to bolster his point: "Media are mere vehicles that deliver instruction but do not influence student achievement any more than the truck that delivers our groceries causes change in our nutrition."[18]

In the end, it was economics that most likely kept PLATO from realizing its potential in the classroom. Bitzer and his team were never able to get the cost per instructional hour down to a point where it made financial sense. In 1976, the project was sold to mainframe computer maker Computer Data Corporation where it did well for a decade before being sold to a series of other companies, most recently Edmentum. The University of Illinois created a separate version of PLATO in 1994, called NovaNet, which was sold to textbook behemoth Pearson, which incorporated it into the Pearson Digital Learning division.[19]

So was PLATO a success? From a commercial standpoint, the answer is mixed. PLATO was used for half a century and is still sold today. From that perspective, Don Bitzer sees it as a success, although his lofty ideals of fundamentally changing education were never really achieved. He should, however, be proud when he puts his engineer's pocket-protector on at how many of PLATO's innovations live on, in the plasma television, pixel-based displays, touch screens, online forums, email, instant messaging, and multiplayer games. The concepts of answer judging and the ability for teachers to create their own courseware were ahead of their time, and they are still not incorporated in most modern learning tools.

Seymour Papert's Logo

Much as the Sputnik crisis drove the 1960s reactive commercialization of educational television and teaching machines, a 1983 report from Ronald Reagan's National Commission on Excellence in Education, *A Nation at Risk*, sounded the alarm for yet another intervention in America's schools. This time, personal computers were the white knights dispatched to rescue the flailing students from academic failure. In response to the report, funding for classroom computers became available, and schools began to buy computers for teachers to use in their classrooms.[20]

The educator Robert Taylor has identified three primary ways computers were used in these early classrooms: as tool, tutor, or tutee. As a *tool*, the computer supported students in performing an unrelated learning goal, such as using a word processor to write a paper. As *tutor*, the computer acted like a traditional teaching machine, imparting curricular content didactically. Finally, as a *tutee*, the computer became the *subject* of programming rather than the *deliverer* of programmed content. Seymour Papert's innovative, and at times controversial, Logo movement became the most popular example of the tutee genre.[21]

As a young boy in Pretoria, South Africa, Papert was strongly drawn toward cars and all things mechanical. He was especially entranced by the way that gears meshed with one another, their rotation always in proportion to their relative size—a smaller gear requiring more turns to rotate than a larger gear, and vice-versa. When he was in lower school, the relationship between these gears provided Papert with a physical model to explore and truly understand the abstract ideas behind multiplying numbers. Later, he was able to extend that simple, but physically observable, understanding about the relationship between the number of cogs in each gear into more abstract concepts, including physically grasping the concept of equations with two variables, such as $3x + 4y = 10$.[22]

Perhaps because of his fascination with gears, Papert ultimately became a mathematician, receiving two PhDs in mathematics: the first in 1952, at the University of the Witwatersrand, in Johannesburg, South Africa, and the second in 1958 at Cambridge University. But while working as a researcher in Paris, Papert attended a lecture by the Swiss developmental psychologist Jean Piaget that would dramatically change the course of his work. Piaget invited Papert to join him at the University of Geneva, and he became one of Piaget's most successful protégés. Over the course of his four-year "apprenticeship," his theoretical outlook on children's learning was fully transformed. Papert (figure 4.5) ultimately joined the faculty of MIT where he became immersed in the emerging world of mini and microcomputers.[23]

Once again, Papert was able to extend the concept of gears, this time as a metaphor for learning: a transitional object can not only attach new knowledge to what a learner already knows, but it can also extrapolate into even more complex understanding. For Papert, the emerging personal computer, with its ability to take on an unlimited number of forms, was an object-to-think-with, a veritable Trojan horse.[24]

Papert conceived of "teaching machines" serving in a much different role than anyone from John Heyl Vincent to Don Bitzer might have predicted. The earlier devices were designed to teach a carefully prescribed curriculum by providing guided access to small bits of content and extracting responses from the learner to reinforce that learning. In contrast, Papert wanted to provide students with a simplified environment that required them to authentically learn that same content while in pursuit of solving problems. To him, the nascent computer was the ultimate erector set, offering a highly interactive environment for students to learn by solving micro problems in the process of doing a macro activity.

Papert believed that getting kids to program was the key for them to learning higher-level skills, something the previous generations of teaching machines could not deliver. And his ideas were influential in the 1980s in getting schools to adopt the emerging personal computer in this new

Figure 4.5. Seymour Papert, 1988.
Courtesy L. Barry Hetherington

manner. Strongly influenced by his work with Piaget, Papert developed *constructionism*, a theoretical framework for his approach to learning, and he introduced the Logo computer language as a tool children could use to learn through programming.

Constructionism and Constructivism

Any exploration of Papert's ideas on teaching and learning must begin with Jean Piaget's theory of constructivism. Piaget had strong ideas about how children viewed the world they inhabited. He envisioned them not merely as small adults but as distinct beings with age-related and fundamentally different views of their environment. For Piaget, successful education began with an understanding that children had a set of evolving theories based on direct experience related to their previous experiences and understanding. This, in effect, was how children created meaning. In order to expand upon current understanding, children need to discover for themselves the "error of their ways" and make connections based on their own experience rather than learning by being told directly.[25] Piaget believed that children were "builders of their own intellectual structures" without any need for formal instruction, that education came from the bottom up, not the top down, and that learning occurs without a formal curriculum and without deliberate teaching.[26]

Papert diverged from Piaget in subtle but important ways. Although both men thought that all new knowledge was self-constructed, Piaget held that children learned higher-level formal and abstract ideas from concrete interactions, whereas Papert believed the opposite. Papert's constructionism posits that the concrete instance and the abstract idea it represents are part of the same continuum and should be considered together: "Becoming one with the object under study is a key to learning."[27]

This is in stark contrast with the reductionist methods used in the previous teaching machines, where larger ideas were chopped up into smaller, more digestible chunks, and the larger abstract or gestalt emerged from the pieces. Papert, by contrast, created simplified environments he called *microworlds*, where instead of leading the student to the answer in small steps, he set up a simplified environment that was constrained for exploring some specific problem in which students would construct their own solutions.[28] In constructionism, the teacher's role is to define a problem that encompasses the content to be learned, construct an environment that will facilitate solving the problem through exploration and inquiry, and provide gentle support for the student's exploration of that environment.

Logo: A Programming Language for Kids

In the 1960s and '70s, the Cambridge research firm Bolt, Beranek and Newman (BBN) was a hotbed of innovation in the world of computing, eventually developing the packet-switching technology that formed the basis of the Internet. While at BBN as a researcher in 1967, Papert helped develop a new computer language called Logo, which children could use to explore these microworlds. Logo was based on Lisp, a popular language used in artificial intelligence applications at the time. Eventually, Logo would be developed for all of the popular personal computers of the day.[29]

Papert initially began to use Logo as a vehicle to test his constructionist ideas with young children. He used an innovative graphical technique, which he called *turtle graphics*, to make the abstract ideas of Cartesian geometry more manipulatable. A likeness of a turtle could be moved about the computer screen by using simple relative commands, such as "move forward 10 steps" and "turn right 90 degrees." A "pen" could begin and stop drawing to create a graphical record of the turtle's motion on the screen. Controlling the turtle was thought to be intuitive for children because they could imagine themselves as the turtle moving through space. The turtle's movement commands could be combined to create more complex shapes and drawings, and algorithmic control structures such as "repeat" made complex tasks easier.[30]

To teach a lesson using Logo, the teacher first assigns the student a problem to solve, such as "draw a flower" (figure 4.6). The student then divides the overall problem into a series of smaller, solvable subproblems, called *procedures*, as steps needed to solve the larger problem: draw an arc, draw a petal, draw the bulb, draw the flower. This made the overall process less daunting; as one seventh grader said, "See, all my procedures are mind-sized bites." Each procedure was then made up of the Logo commands to solve that one aspect of the overall problem. Critical to the process was the ability to make mistakes (and learn from them), the programming construct of *debugging.*[31]

In 1980, Papert outlined his ideas on computer-based learning environments, microworlds, and learning in his best-selling book, *Mindstorms*, which became very popular as educators and policymakers alike tried to understand the implications of the computer in learning and the role of the computer in creating meaning. With computers becoming more common in the classroom, some teachers, inspired by *Mindstorms*, adopted Papert's constructionist approach, using Logo to teach their students. A Logo community flourished, with Papert serving as its most vocal spokesperson, and like the innovators of teaching machines before him, Papert made optimistic statements about Logo's effectiveness in teaching higher-level thinking skills.

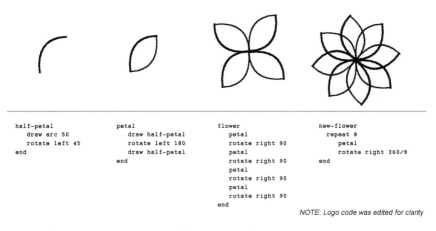

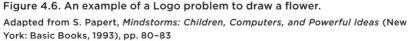

NOTE: Logo code was edited for clarity

Figure 4.6. An example of a Logo problem to draw a flower.
Adapted from S. Papert, *Mindstorms: Children, Computers, and Powerful Ideas* (New York: Basic Books, 1993), pp. 80–83.

In spite of the rhetoric, there was considerable controversy about Logo's ability to actually improve those elusive higher-level thinking skills. In 1984, an article in *Psychology Today* reported on a study critical of Logo's ability to show results in some tasks that presumed to show evidence of higher-level thinking. Researchers who conducted the study at Bank Street College's Center of Children and Technology concluded, "Logo promises more than it has delivered." Interest in using Logo in the classroom began to wane.[32]

Almost four decades after he initially developed Logo, Seymour Papert was still optimistic that schools would eventually adopt Logo, or something like it. Even though the impact might be small, the constructionist/constructivist ideas were beginning to take hold. Logo may not be used in schools with much frequency, but the new vocabularies in American education— such as *twentieth-century skills, higher-order thinking,* and *critical-thinking skills*—reflect the impact of Papert's student-centered and inquiry-based approaches to pedagogy.[33]

The biggest difference between the constructionist approach and that of previous teaching machines is that Papert put the student, rather than the instructor, squarely in control of the learning process. The student controls the pace of instruction according to his or her abilities and must find a mastery-level solution to the problem in order to proceed to the next challenge. That ultimate solution is attained by solving a series of smaller-sized tasks, but the student chooses his or her own path toward solving the overall problem and is personally responsible for subdividing the larger goal into manageable chunks. Finally, the process of debugging Logo provides a kind of successive approximation, in the Skinnerian sense of shaping of small actions toward a larger goal. Papert commented that a first grader who tried to rotate a turtle 270 degrees "understood enough (and scarcely enough) to produce an action, an action interesting enough to start a movement among the first graders. He did not understand what 270 means. I am not sure that the number 270 in itself meant very much to him, let alone 270 degrees, but this is how real learning happens. You understand just enough to get going, to do something and to learn by doing and by discovery."[34]

The CD-ROM Revolution

The CD-ROM, introduced in mid-1980s, offered an inexpensive way to distribute a large amount of digital content (up to 700MB) to a mass audience. These disks enabled a new genre of computer applications called *edutainment*, which blurred the line between a game and a tool for learning and were graphically rich and fun for kids. Previously, delivering an application containing this amount of information required hundreds of bulky and expensive floppy disks that needed to be painstakingly loaded one by one to the computer's hard drive. CD-ROMs freed developers to use attractive graphics, animation, video, and audio to create compelling multimedia experiences that they could not practically deliver before.

Many of these programs, such Reader Rabbit, Math Blaster, and the JumpStart series, employed gamified* versions of drill and practice activities to learn math, spelling, and vocabulary. But excellent simulation-style games also emerged, including SimCity, Civilization, and The Oregon Trail, which offered players a more exploratory and self-guided environment, more aligned with Papert's constructivist/constructionist approach. All of these games were adopted by parents looking to give their kids an edge, and they were routinely used as fodder for the computers that were beginning to populate American classrooms.

---

*Gamification refers to the process of adding gamelike attributes to nongame activities, such as earning points and virtual "badges" for progress through the activity. It has a somewhat pejorative connotation with developers.

There has been a paucity of hard research on the effectiveness of edutainment programs, so it's not clear whether these applications have any real positive effects on learning. Researchers informally looked at how students engaged with the Oregon Trail program, which provided an attractive historical simulation of homesteaders traveling by wagon train from the Missouri River to Oregon in 1848. When properly supervised, students could gain valuable insight into pioneer life, but left to their own devices, they tended to concentrate more on getting through the game as quickly as possible, as opposed to thoughtfully exploring the game's microworld with its rich historical content. Students resorted to trial-and-error strategies rather than thinking through the problems in a thoughtful way. In short, they tended to interact with the program in ways that bypassed some or all of the educational objectives; they were more focused on the game-specific (and fun) elements of the program.[35]

Games were not the only application the new disks enabled. Microsoft's president Bill Gates saw the CD-ROM as a perfect vehicle to provide a digital alternative to bulky and expensive sets of encyclopedia volumes. In the summer of 1985, Microsoft approached the esteemed but financially struggling Encyclopaedia Britannica to license their content, but in a classic example straight out of the innovator's dilemma,* the company demurred, saying it had "no plans to be on a home computer. And since the market is so small—only 4 or 5 percent of households have computers—we would not want to hurt our traditional way of selling."[36]

In 1989, Microsoft purchased Britannica's nearly bankrupt competitor, *Funk & Wagnall's New Encyclopedia*, added a significant amount of compelling multimedia content, and released it on CD-ROM in 1993 under the name *Encarta*. The new digital format was more engaging and searchable than the print version, and it forced Britannica to release its own digital version in 1995; in 2010, Britannica ceased publication of its venerable print version.[37]

*The *innovator's dilemma* was proposed by Harvard Business School professor Clayton Christensen to explain why market incumbents fail to adopt disruptive change by new innovations: because they don't want the new innovation to interfere with their current business activities even though ignoring them may prove disastrous. See C. Christensen, *The Innovator's Dilemma: When New Technologies Cause Great Firms to Fail* (Boston: Harvard Business School Press, 1997).

CD-ROM-based edutainment games had a meteoric rise, with over $500 million in sales at their peak in 2000, and an equally swift fall, with sales plummeting to $152 million by 2004.[38] There are several reasons for the decline, but clearly the emergence of the Internet played a large role. Instead of having to provide content on the limited space of the CD-ROM, as large as it was, Web sites could deliver an unlimited variety on demand, often for free. CD-ROMs needed to be purchased in a physical store, making them less accessible and competitive with the emerging online games.[39]

Serious Games: Game-Based Learning

By the turn of the twenty-first century, video games were an entrenched part of the average American childhood. Parents, educators, and trainers marveled at the hours kids spent engrossed within them and wondered if that rapture might be applied toward their own learning objectives. The serious games movement, also known as game-based learning, sought to create games that had defined learning outcomes. In serious games, the addition of pedagogy makes a game serious, but the pedagogical element should work in concert with the game's narrative in order for it to be both useful and appealing.

Ben Sawyer is the unofficial spokesman for the serious games movement, and he is a combination of theorist, game developer, and also the movement's staunchest advocate. In 2002, he founded the Serious Games Conference, and in 2004 the Games for Health Conference, which focuses on games targeted toward health issues. These two conferences have provided a powerful nexus for academics, researchers, developers, and their funders to create a community to explore the use of gaming in a wide range of applications, from education and edutainment to simulations and social impact.[40]

Sawyer believes that all games are serious and that video games have unique traits. If exploited properly, they can encourage a dialogue between the player and the developer. Serious games can expose the player to "accelerated encounters," early opportunities to experience a wide variety of sophisticated ideas. He tells the story of his nine-year-old son learning what a mortgage was in the process of playing a game and how this kind of early encounter forms a basis for more sophisticated understandings over time.[41]

There has been much theorizing about the potential value of games in education. On the academic side, the psycholinguist James Paul Gee made a thoughtful exploration of video games to understand how they might provide some insight into the educational process. He spent a year actively playing a number of educational and noneducational video games and was able to extract a set of important learning principles he found in them, things that made them both appealing and instructive. The thirty-six principles Gee identified are clustered around three groupings; *situated cognition*, where thinking happens in the head and in the environment; *new literacy studies*, where learning has political, historic, and economic implications; and *connectivism*, which recognizes our brains for their powerful pattern-matching capabilities.[42]

On the corporate and military training side, writer and corporate game developer Marc Prensky has been a vocal advocate for using games in learning. A man known for his provocative statements, Prensky claims that today's children are fundamentally different from children of previous generations because they have grown up immersed in the digital technologies of computers, video games, and the Internet. He believes that these *digital natives* are having their brains wired differently from the *digital immigrants*, such as their teachers, and they need to be taught differently.[43] Whether that is indeed true is the subject of much debate (I am personally skeptical), but it has brought considerable interest from educators into using game dynamics to support learning.

To understand serious games, it is useful to define the elements that make up any kind of game, whether they use cards, boards, parties, or video as their vehicle. According to game developers David Michael and Sande Chen, the following characteristics are evident in successful games: "voluntary activity, obviously separate from real life, creating an imaginary world that may or may not have any relation to real life and that absorbs the player's full attention. Games are played out within a specific time and place, are played according to established rules, and create social groups out of their players." Obviously, in most serious games, the voluntary aspect of a successful game is missing when it is assigned. In a survey of serious game developers, educators, and researchers, 82 percent of the participants rated the entertainment value of the game to be of *high importance*.[44]

Serious games were initially embraced by the military. At first they preferred to call them *simulations*, ostensibly to lend an air of gravity to the enterprise and justify the vast amount of money directed toward them—some $4 billion a year, for example, to develop deeply immersive 3-D simulations, many of which are game-based. Such games are used to train soldiers, with the benefits being improved hand-eye coordination, social skills, and cross-cultural sensitivity, as well as better multitasking and better teamwork skills in environments with constrained communication.[45] Serious games later began to be used in the healthcare industry, and by governments and non-governmental organizations alike. They are used educationally for simulations such as surgical training and for teaching patients new skills and instilling habits, such as better nutrition or diabetes control. Education has been a tougher market for serious games to enter, whether it is a hang-over from the edutainment era or because of ineffective marketing or per-haps due to the lack of hard evidence that serious games produce improved learning outcomes.[46]

Serious games developer Dov Jacobson is an artist and technologist (a combination that was rarer in the 1980s than it is now) who develops games for the military and health industries at his Atlanta-based company GamesThatWork.[47] He began his career in Los Angeles as a film animator, creating the beautiful and elaborate animations of planets for Carl Sagan's *Cosmos* series on PBS. Jacobson came back to New York to develop games that ran on Time Warner's set-top boxes for their growing cable television network. In one of the most productive collaborations I ever had, Dov and I worked together in the 1980s creating animation software on the emer-gent IBM PC for professional artists and animators. But games were always his first love, and in 1993, he joined Turner Broadcasting as an executive to develop Turner Interactive, making games such as the successful Civil War and Dinotopia titles.

Jacobson was sponsored by the National Institutes for Health (NIH) to create a game that would help children learn to brush their teeth better, which is ironic, since Jacobson's father was a dentist. The resulting game adapts the remote control from Nintendo's popular Wii® game console (colloquially called the Wiimote) to sense how kids were brushing and uses gaming techniques to teach an accepted brushing method. The Brush Up game played music, which the kids brushed their teeth to while receiving visual, audio, haptic,* and tactile feedback as to how they were doing (fig-ure 4.7). In a preliminary study of the effectiveness of the game, Jacobson

---

Haptic technology uses the sense of touch by applying forces such as, vibrations, or motions to the user.

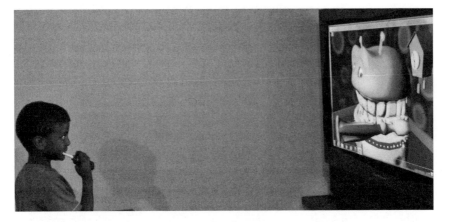

Figure 4.7. Teaching kids to brush with the *Brush Up* game.
Courtesy of GamesThatWork.com

found that the kids improved their brushing performance three-fold after 14 plays.

In serious games we see many of the same positive attributes found in the other teaching machines examined so far: learners proceed at their own pace through the game in small steps. Like Papert's Logo, they are immersed in a constrained environment where specific objectives are defined and learners must navigate through that microworld on their own. Their actions receive immediate feedback, and they must completely master a sub-problem before moving on to the next.

As was the case with edutainment CD-ROMs, almost no hard research that has tested the effectiveness of serious games, and what evidence exists is anecdotal. But researchers have found that games can support development of a number of skills prized in education and industry, such as strategic thinking, planning, communication, collaboration, group decision making, and negotiating.[48]

The mixture of education and entertainment may not have always worked in practice. Some educators have likened creating an educational game to the challenge of baking a healthy, but tasty cake. It's easy to make a delicious sugar- and butter-laden cake (a fun game) or a heart-healthy but bland cake made from oat germ and sawdust (educational content), but it's tough to make one that satisfies both needs. One approach is to take the cake (pure entertainment) and inject some vitamins into it (educational content), the tack taken by most edutainment games. Alternatively, one can take a bland cake (educational content) and add food coloring (gamification features) to make it look like a tasty cake. It's healthy but still tastes awful (educational, but not fun to play).[49]

Intelligent Teaching Machines

As computers became more affordable and accessible, an industry supporting computer-aided instruction sprang up; for the most part, these systems tended to be better versions of the programmed instruction teaching machines, but in more accessible and flexible packaging. The interactive capacities of the computer were not really harnessed to their fullest; rather, software simply delivered content and assessed student responses using quizzes and tests. Based on those assessments, students were either passed on to the next unit to be learned or sent back for remedial instruction and practice.

Unfortunately, as useful as it was to alert learners when they made mistakes, these CAI programs typically delivered the remedial instruction in exactly the same way the original instruction, with no change based on the kind of error the student actually made. This meant there was no guarantee that repeating the same instruction would keep the student from having the same problems the next time around. Researchers began to look into "a more sensitive" method to diagnose not merely if answers were wrong but *why* they were wrong. This concept of accurate error diagnosis is fundamental to all successful tutoring, and developers began to incorporate the understanding of the nature of errors into a new generation of intelligent teaching machines.[50]

While the definition of an intelligent tool is the subject of much debate, there was some consensus, at least in the context of education, that "a system must *behave* intelligently, not actually *be* intelligent, like a human," according to the psychologist Valerie Shute. The philosophical and technological framework the researchers used to build these new intelligent tools was the emerging field of artificial intelligence.[51] Fueled by large grants from the military and government in the 1960s and 1970s, AI researchers made sweeping claims about the imminent arrival of machines that could "think," which never came true. AI's credibility was crippled by its own hubris about finding the next big thing. As with many examples of making grandiose promises while under-delivering, funding sources and the pub-

lic grew weary of the unrealized dreams and dismissed the field as a failure, but I believe that to give up on AI entirely would be a mistake in the
long run.[52]

Granted, we do not have the kind of intelligent computers such as HAL
from Stanley Kubrick's 1968 film *2001: A Space Odyssey*, but the work in
artificial intelligence has made an impact in less dramatic, but equally
valuable, ways. These include natural language processing, expert systems
for medical diagnoses, fraud detection, Google, and many other big-data
applications. Seymour Papert, who was instrumental in early artificial intelligence research, defined AI as "extending the capacity of machines to
perform functions that would be intelligent if performed by people." And
he cautioned, "In order to construct such machines, it is usually necessary
to reflect not only on the nature of machines but on the nature of the intelligent functions to be performed." Papert believed that artificial intelligence
was an opportunity to make these abstract ideas more concrete.[53]

Some investigators looked at the knowledge-modeling techniques pioneered by earlier AI work and began to apply them to the older, simpler
CAI systems in order to make them act more like human tutors. *Knowledge
modeling* is a way to organize curricular content by dividing it into a series
of smaller, but conceptually interconnected, elements. This view is fundamentally different from the way previous teaching machines divided content
into smaller portions that flowed linearly from one to the next; instead, it
conceives of portions having multiple connections to other concepts in a
web-like fashion (figure 4.8).

Reaching the effectiveness of one-to-one human tutoring has been the
gold standard of educational technology ever since 1984, when educational
psychologist Benjamin Bloom found in a series of studies that one-to-one
tutoring could achieve a two-sigma improvement over traditional classroom
teaching (the equivalent of jumping from 500 to 700 on the SAT test).[54] AI
researchers regarded the tutorial pedagogical model as the most effective
technique to emulate, and they began to develop intelligent tutoring systems that could behave (and hopefully perform) like human tutors.

Intelligent Tutoring Systems

ITS designs differ significantly from their computer-driven predecessors. Rather than the one-size-fits-all strategy of delivering content to
a passive learner, ITS designs are able to customize the learning experience

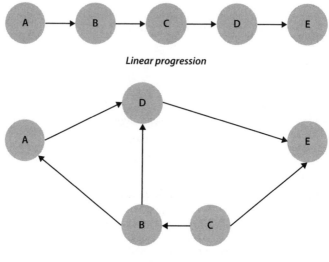

Linear progression

Knowledge model

Figure 4.8. Linear progression versus knowledge model.

the student receives based on factors such as preexisting knowledge, learning style, and the student's progress through the content material.

There are a considerable variety of intelligent tutoring systems, but most share the same overarching organizational structure. A typical ITS will contain a number of conceptual components, or models, that interact with one another. The *content model* contains a web-like mapping of the content to be learned, defining the prerequisites and dependencies between content elements. The *student model* is unique to each learner and works in parallel with the content model to record what the student does and does not yet understand. Finally, there is a method of delivering the instruction to the learner, known as the *pedagogical model*.[55]

Most ITSs begin the instructional process by determining what the student already knows, typically through an assessment. The system then continues to update the student model status as instruction occurs. Comparing what the student needs to know with what she already knows (i.e., comparing the student model with the content model), it delivers the pedagogically appropriate unit of instruction to the student (figure 4.9).[56]

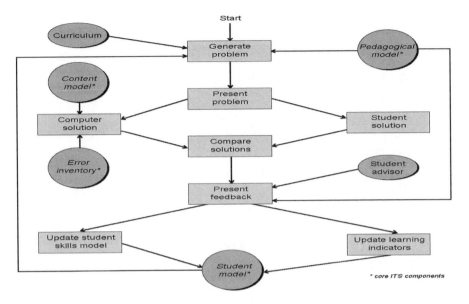

Figure 4.9. Diagram of a typical ITS.
Adapted from V. Shute and J. Psotka, "Intelligent Tutoring Systems: Past, Present and Future," in *Handbook of Research on Educational Communications and Technology*, ed. D. Jonassen (New York: Macmillan Library Reference, 1996)

The instruction is often embedded with assessment or highly interactive problem-solving capabilities so that the student model is dynamically updated to always reflect the student's current knowledge level. The ITS takes advantage of the granularity of the content being so fine and well-matched to the student model that just the right amount of remediation is offered, theoretically yielding shorter learning times.[57]

The first ITS to use a content model to embody the curriculum to be taught was developed by the computer scientist Jaime Carbonell in 1969. His SCHOLAR program used a network for representing knowledge about Latin American geography, and SCHOLAR interacted with the learner using a kind of Socratic dialogue technique that employed preprogrammed templates and relatively crude word recognition.[58]

In 1982, John Seeley Brown at Xerox's PARC research group developed WEST, which was based on the popular board game of the time, How the

West Was Won. WEST used a coaching strategy (i.e., "sage on the side") for students to interactively solve arithmetic problems by moving pieces on a virtual board. The system diagnosed the student's responses and offered remediation to correct for any deficits.[59]

One of the most successful efforts, at least in terms of its longevity, is Carnegie Mellon University's series of mathematics tutors for middle schoolers. Psychology and computer science professor John Anderson was able to marry ITS engineering to a cognitive science theory for simulating and understanding human cognition, called the ACT* theory of learning.[60] This theory was used to undergird many successful ITS programs in the early 1980s for teaching the Lisp computer programming, called the Lisp Tutor, and ultimately the successful geometry and algebra tutors, which are sold today by Carnegie Learning Corporation.[61]

Educational psychologist Valerie Shute developed a popular series of computer modules in 1994 that used an allusion to the "Church Lady" from the popular Dana Carvey skit on NBC's *Saturday Night Live* to teach introductory statistics.[62] Portions of Stat Lady's student model design were influenced by Anderson's ACT theory. Stat Lady was innovative beyond its humorous digitally animated host, in that the student model was very tightly aligned to the content model and was coded into procedural, symbolic, and conceptual elements and tracked with a very fine level of granularity in order to deliver appropriate curriculum sequencing and remediation to the student at precisely the most valuable time.[63]

A new generation of systems that took advantage of the Internet's ability to deliver intelligent instruction began to emerge in Europe during the mid-1990s. While paying homage to their historical ITS roots, their developers began to exploit some of the adaptivity the World Wide Web could offer. An alphabet soup of acronyms followed (AES, AWBES, AHS, AHA, AIF . . .), as researchers scrambled to use the rapidly evolving Internet infrastructure to deliver highly interactive instruction over the Web. The "A" in all the acronyms stands for *adaptive*, meaning a student model is embedded into the design to adapt the instruction according to the preexisting knowledge, progress, and learning style of the student.

---

*ACT is short for "adaptive control of thought."

Can Intelligent Tutoring Systems Teach?

In spite of the lack of visibility of ITS systems outside the rarified air of university research labs, there is a modest amount of research suggesting that intelligent tutoring systems can achieve remarkable increases in student learning over traditional classroom instruction in the real world. As with the mechanical teaching machines of Pressey and Skinner, this increase can be measured as reduced time on task, as well as higher scores on post-tests.

For example, an ITS tutor designed to teach the Lisp computer language, called LISPITS, was evaluated in three different learning environments: one-to-one human instruction, working with a printed workbook, and using LISPITS. All three groups performed equally well on the post-test, but the difference in times required to reach this mastery were significant: the human-tutored students finished in 12 hours, the students who used the LISPITS program finished in 15 hours, and the students who used the workbook finished last, after 28 hours.[64]

Shute conducted a study of Stat Lady's performance as compared with the same introductory statistics material taught in a traditional classroom, and she found the much sought-after two-sigma improvement with the ITS.[65] Sherlock, an ITS designed to teach field maintenance procedures to Air Force ground crew mechanics on F-16 fighters, was able to yield the same level of competency after 20–25 hours of instruction as those who took traditional training attained over four years.[66] Carnegie Learning Corporation reported that students utilizing its algebra I tutor performed 85 percent better on assessments of complex problem solving skills, 14 percent better on basic mathematics skills, and 30 percent better on TIMSS* assessments.[67]

Why Intelligent Tutoring Systems Have Not Flourished

Intelligent tutoring systems have clearly not lived up to their potential, at least when judged by their adoption by the education community, in spite of seeming to have the right combination of features. But it

*The Trends in International Mathematics and Science Study (TIMSS) is a standardized test that provides reliable and timely data on the mathematics and science achievement of U.S. fourth- and eighth-grade students compared with students in other countries.

would be unfair to discount some 30 years of research for what appears to be issues of execution. The results of the studies on the efficacy of ITSs suggest that they can be effective in improving student learning, but several factors have aligned to deliver "defeat from the jaws of victory."

Perhaps the most important hurdle to overcome is the difficulty in authoring courseware used by ITS programs. Historically, most systems had their content "hard-coded" into the ITS software, which had to be done by skilled programmers at great expense. This also meant that instructors and other subject matter experts were not able to participate directly in the development of the content portions of the systems. There also has been inflexibility in the varieties of pedagogical approaches to instruction, where different instructional approaches could be used at more appropriate times.[68]

Diagnosing wrong answers turns out to be an exceedingly difficult, time-consuming, and expensive problem to solve; it requires tediously connecting by hand a large number of potential wrong answers with specific remedial instruction. For example, there are over 600 possible misconceptions about early addition and multiplication alone, which has a narrowly defined scope. For more complicated topics such as physics, the number of misconceptions would be completely overwhelming. In the 1960s teaching machines era, Norman Crowder also found this a problem while implementing his simpler teaching machine's branching techniques. Although it was possible for instruction authors to support wrong-answer remediation, few actually ever did.[69]

According to intelligent tutoring system pioneer Peter Brusilovsky, more recent research efforts are using a big-data* approach with machine-learning and statistical techniques to automatically supplement some of the tuning of the weights of content models. Up to this point, big-data approaches have been useful in assessing affect, such as student frustration and protection against students' "gaming the system," but he is optimistic about the role it will play in instruction in future systems. Already, companies such as Knewton and the Khan Academy are employing many of these hybrid approaches in their systems.

---

*Big data is the newly emergent field where large amounts of data are "mined" for correlations and patterns using techniques such as machine learning, statistical regression, and Bayesian inference.

Making Sense of the Computer as a Teaching Machine

The computer has so much promise as the ultimate teaching machine, certainly when compared with books, the electro-mechanical devices of Pressey and Skinner, and the more didactic techniques such as radio, TV, film, and Internet videos. The computer can deliver an almost unlimited amount of engaging, media-rich material in the blink of an eye, engage in a highly interactive and reflexive relationship with the learner, provide instantaneous feedback to questions and responses, and potentially help a student learn faster and easier than most other forms of instruction, with the exception of one-to-one tutoring.

Part of the problem may be McLuhan-esque in nature. Like all new kinds of media that mimic the forms that have preceded it, the computer has been called upon to teach using methodologies that may not take advantage of all of its computational affordances. Another issue is social and cultural. The American classroom was designed primarily for whole-class activities led by an instructor. Engaging with a computer is fundamentally a one-to-one activity, and that presents a practical implementation conflict.

The grandfathers of computer-based instruction, PLATO and Carnegie Learning, have been delivering computer-based instruction for decades, albeit with relatively modest success, but educators have not widely adopted these systems. Seymour Papert's Logo had a spark of interest from educators in the 1980s, but its constructivist/constructionist nature, which makes it a great tool for inquiry and learning, also makes it slower to teach with the content specificity required in an ever-increasingly assessment-driven school environment.

The edutainment craze and serious games movement also failed to have much of an impact. One of the reasons may echo why educational films did not take hold. Games specifically developed for teaching had to live with much smaller budgets than modern commercial video-game productions, whose budgets rival those of feature films, yet they were still being judged by the higher standards of the commercial enterprises. The constructivist/constructionist nature of games makes them prey to some of the same pressures as Logo, where the learning targets are equally indirect.

In thinking about ITS, it is hard to envision a potentially more effective system for instruction. Such systems contain a semantically connected conceptualization of the content to be taught, a way of knowing what the learner does and doesn't understand, and a delivery method that adapts that instruction accordingly. It would appear that the early systems were not executed well enough to become mainstream, but they should, nonetheless, provide a rich foundation for future teaching machines to draw lessons from, as these systems begin to use the computer's power for more than simply delivering instruction.

So if the computer by itself couldn't produce an effective teaching machine, perhaps a network of them might. The next chapter looks at the Internet and how its ability to instantly connect people, processing, and content has ignited the most recent push to apply technology to education.

5

From the Cloud

Yogi Berra once said, "Prediction is very hard, especially about the future,"[1] and writing about recent developments is tantamount to making predictions. With a generation or more of history behind the teaching machines explored thus far, the impact and future trajectories are easier to assess than the still-unfolding stories in this chapter. With that caveat, it is becoming clear that the Internet is the most powerful environment for teaching to date. Until now, we have predominantly seen "filmed plays" that merely take advantage of the frictionless delivery of content or offer more accessible versions of practice and drill applications. Truly interactive applications that couple the power of the modern personal computer with the networked nature of the Web have a great, but largely unrealized, potential.

Cloud computing refers to a new breed of Web-based applications that store data on online servers and then make that information instantly available from any Internet-connected computer, usually using a standard Web browser. The name "cloud" comes from an illustration of a cloud that was used in block diagrams of early Internet-based systems. The computer industry and the popular press use the name as a buzzword for any system in which data are stored on servers and accessed locally.

The progression from early Web-based e-learning applications, through megalithic learning-management systems such as Blackboard and Sakai (which some might argue do not represent a step forward), and on to a new generation of teaching machines, such as the Khan Academy and the unfortunately named massive open online courses (MOOCs), is continuing toward the goal of more effective tools for learning. New efforts are poised to tap some of the potential that computer advocates have long sought, and the developers of PLATO hinted at in 1960.

E-learning and Distance Learning

The e-learning, or distance-learning, movement has its historical roots firmly planted in the correspondence schools of the turn of the twentieth century. Rather than relying on the slow postal service to move printed curricular material, however, modern e-learning providers use the Internet to deliver their content to students as Web pages. These new electronic textbooks have some advantages over their paper-based predecessors. They can provide new content instantly, whenever the learner is ready for it; no need to wait until the next lesson arrives in the afternoon mail.

Lessons are easily and economically displayed in full color and can have a wealth of multimedia attached, including images, video, audio, and interactive elements such as simulations and problem sets. This digital content is instantly searchable, making it easier for the student to go back and review sections as needed. Just as International Correspondence Schools divided courses into smaller units, e-learning providers can potentially create custom paths through their curricula that make the instruction closely fit the learner's goals.[2]

These e-learning solutions harness the Internet to transform traditional instruction in different contexts: higher education, job-specific training, and even K–12 education. Most of these tools deliver a didactic, instructor-driven pedagogical experience aimed at replicating the face-to-face classroom experience. Their main advantage over conventional instruction is their ability to provide access for nontraditional students who are unable to attend classes in person because of work, family, or geography.

Anytime, Anyplace

One of the important advantages of e-learning is that it is not necessary for students and the instructor to be in the same location. There are three possible ways a student can participate in a learning experience: in person, completely online, or in some combination of the two, what is known as a *blended learning environment*. This flexibility makes it easy for a wider range of students to participate, including people who work during traditional school hours, stay-at-home parents, those with physical disabilities, and people in geographically remote locations.[3]

And it's not just place that can be changed in e-learning environments but time as well. Unlike in-person classrooms or the broadcast media of educational radio and television, students do not need to meet at a particular time to take in the lecture with the instructor and other students. On-demand video technology allows students to be free of the temporal restraints of needing to consume the content at an appointed time and place.

The model highlights an important differentiator in types of e-learning systems, its synchronicity. A synchronous course presents the lecture at a particular time, whether in person, online, or both. The advantage is that the students have more of a cohort feeling, and if the system allows it, they can potentially interact with one another or the instructor. Asynchronous courses allow students to view the instructional content at any time that is convenient, but because of the lack of a common time space, they cannot interact with fellow students or the instructor in real-time and must rely on email, chat, and online forums to communicate with one another.[4]

E-learning Economics

The economics of e-learning balance the cost to develop the instruction and the cost of delivering it. In-person and synchronous online lecture and seminar-based classes are inexpensive to create but expensive to deliver because the instructor's time is not leveraged; each time the class is taught, the instructor must be present to teach it. This makes large lecture classes with hundreds of students financially appealing to universities, but such a setting offers little interaction between faculty and students. Smaller seminars, project-based learning, and studio art classes provide the kinds of student-instructor interaction we've come to associate with the traditional college experience, but the cost per student is high (figure 5.1).

Having on-demand videos of classroom lectures lowers the cost of instructional delivery but adds the costs of providing a (hopefully) well-produced video lecture. Just as with large classroom lectures, this method results in a lack of student-instructor interaction, but advocates claim the ability to watch the videos multiple times mitigates this problem. This is one reason why the large lecture university courses are feeling vulnerable to the new video on demand lectures proffered by MOOCs and others.

The holy grail for effective distance learning that can effectively and economically scale probably lies in student-driven and asynchronous learning (the fourth quadrant of the diagram in figure 5.1). There are no good

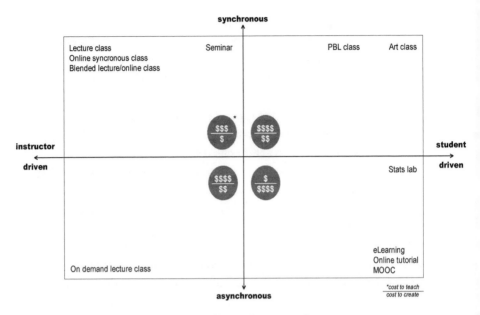

Figure 5.1. Synchronicity versus instruction centering.

examples as yet, but the recent surge in investments in educational technology will most certainly drive development in that direction.

E-learning in Higher Education

Taking a page straight out of the correspondence school playbook,
for-profit universities such as the University of Phoenix, Capella University, and Walden University have emerged to offer nontraditional students
an opportunity to earn accredited undergraduate and graduate degrees using the Internet. Like the postal-based companies a century earlier, these
schools are unabashedly commercial enterprises determined to provide
education to a sector of the population that was not served by more traditional institutions. They provide their own curricular content, offer timely
feedback from instructors, and some even offer physical satellite campuses
for face-to-face classroom instruction.

These schools have provoked much criticism; detractors argue that
they engage in aggressive and predatory sales tactics that take advantage
of veteran benefits and other government programs and commit students to

heavy student loan burdens for an education that may not be worth the price they paid for it.[5] A typical tuition for 120 credits (the usual requirement for a bachelor's degree at most universities) cost $48,000 in 2011 at the University of Phoenix; at a state university it would have cost only $30,000. Couple this with the exceeding low completion rates for all for-profit universities, and they look like an expensive educational option that people who are able to attend in-person classes are forced to consider.[6] In 2010, the University of Phoenix settled a lawsuit for the then unprecedented amount of $78 million over issues surrounding aggressive student recruitment.[7]

In spite of the controversy, the University of Phoenix remains the oldest, largest, and most successful of the for-profit universities. Founded in 1976 by economics professor turned entrepreneur John Sperling with only eight students, it has grown into a $2 billion public company that by 2010 had granted well over 500,000 degrees.[8] In 1989, the university branched out from its brick-and-mortar roots and began offering online classes using the then popular CompuServe online community; it became fully Internet-based in the mid-1990s.

The classes are instructor-led and consist of 10–20 students, giving them a more human touch than completely computerized systems, such as PLATO. Much like the earlier postal correspondence schools, students receive individualized feedback on their assignments and questions through email, online-chat, and discussion forums. The University of Phoenix maintains over 100 campuses across the United States, where student can find face-to-face instruction.

The University of Phoenix maintains its profit advantage over traditional colleges by commoditizing the instruction to achieve better economies of scale. In 2011, Phoenix spent $3,069 per student, as compared with $7,534 in public universities and an astounding $15,215 for private institutions. Courses and curricular materials are developed centrally by a corporate development team and are led by interchangeable instructors.[9]

Public universities are also increasingly looking at distance education programs to serve nontraditional students who cannot attend classes in person. This trend can be traced back to the 1890s, when William Rainey Harper joined the University of Chicago and instituted some of the ideas about correspondence learning that he acquired as the curriculum director for the Chautauqua Institution in upstate New York.[10]

The United Kingdom's Open University is perhaps the most successful distance-learning institution in the world. Started by the British Ministry of Education in 1971, the Open University has delivered instruction through the changing technologies of the times. It has used radio and television to air late-night broadcasts, videos, DVDs, computer modems, and eventually the Internet to provide degree-granting courses to almost 2 million students worldwide. The curricular materials are made freely available, but the cost to earn a four-year bachelor's degree is approximately $25,000.[11]

E-learning in K–12 and Industry

For the obvious reason that we provide and, in fact, require free face-to-face education for all children in America, e-learning is less commonly used in K–12 education settings, but some applications have been developed to meet specific needs. Many schools do not have teachers able to teach less common subjects, such as foreign languages or advanced math and science topics, so schools have reached out to e-learning providers to fill those needs via the Internet. In addition, parents looking to better prepare their children for high-stakes tests such as the SAT can choose among for-profit test-prep sites on the Internet.

As more and more parents chose to home school their children, markets evolved to provide them with curriculum and educational resources and companies developed e-learning tools to cater to them. Perhaps the best-known company is K12.com, initially led by William Bennett, Ronald Reagan's education secretary. The company offers a full curriculum, from math to music, and uses a simple online textbook in which content is divided into small chunks and displayed on the screen, with occasional questions to answer or problems to solve. A simple individualized learning plan guides students through the curriculum.[12]

Employee training is a huge budget item for American corporations, with an astounding $126 billion spent in 2009 alone,[13] so it's not surprising that e-learning is an important component in corporate training departments, which have moved away from face-to-face training because of the cost and interruption to the workday. Corporate e-learning tends to be different from the e-learning done in educational institutions. The focus is more on learner-centered experiences that are highly mediated by technology, as opposed to the instructor-led, simulated-classroom-environment model embraced by schools.[14]

Learning Management Systems

A learning management system (LMS) is a network-based infrastructure to deliver and manage curricular content, communication, grading, and administration of courses; it is used extensively in traditional face-to-face classrooms and distance-learning environments alike.[15] Even though the LMS technically does not fit the definition of a teaching machine, its ubiquity and role as the tool-of-choice in technology-mediated instruction means it cannot be ignored. Although Blackboard.com dominates the commercial front, it has competition in the open-source Moodle and Sakai systems. These offer less robust pedagogical support than many educators would want, but the open nature of their architectures make them potential candidates for development along those lines in the future.

Modern learning management systems are browser-based Internet applications that provide several functions integrated within a single password-protected Web site. If the grandfathers of distance-learning systems such as the Open University and the University of Phoenix were Chautauquas and correspondence schools, then the modern learning management systems can trace their lineage from the computer-based corporate training systems that emerged in the 1990s and grew in popularity as the Internet grew ubiquitous.

LMSs provide four major functions:

1. Their primary role is to facilitate the efficient and secure delivery of curricular content, learning resources, and links to Internet-based resources.
2. They enable both synchronous and asynchronous ways for students and instructors to communicate with one another, using chat, email, instant messaging, and discussion forums.
3. They offer easy mechanisms for student assessment, such as quizzes or drop boxes where students can submit written work.
4. They provide a simple way to administer the class, with integrated calendars, and syllabi.[16]

In some ways, an LMS democratizes the Internet for instructors, making it easy for them to add Web-accessible content without needing to know arcane HTML coding or to manage their own Web site. Instructors can personally create simple instructional sequences of content that can contain text, images, and video and can be interlaced with quizzes and other assessments in a relatively formative manner.[17] Unfortunately, rather than creating richer curricular resources, most instructors tend to use learning management systems as administrative and content delivery tools for more efficiently managing their courses, with one educator commenting that LMSs have become "little more than storage facilities for lecture notes and Power-Point presentations."[18]

Choosing an LMS is a high-stakes and high-risk decision for a university. The integration into the university's infrastructure is a time-consuming and expensive proposition. Commercial LMS software is expensive to license, and using open-source software can be equally expensive in terms of the amount of support staff required to customize it into the university infrastructure for things like class enrollment and grading. Universities find the lure of the LMS seductive because of the access, costs, and quality improvements they hope to find. The systems offer an increased economy of scale and efficiency in administering instruction, and, importantly, students have come to expect that their university will have a robust learning management system. Indeed, even their high schools likely had some form of LMS.[19]

Criticisms of Learning Management Systems

Of course, just because the majority of learning institutions have adopted learning management systems wholesale does not mean that these systems are not without their critics. Some have taken issues with the time-oriented, teacher-centric, and closed nature of LMS implementations.[20] Most LMSs adopt a militaristic command-and-control style of course management that is antithetical to the more constructivist approach popular among today's instructors. While LMSs are theoretically neutral about pedagogy, in practice they tend to reinforce didactic, information-transmission pedagogical models. Their very design and implementation have a big influence on the nature of instruction, particularly with less-experienced instructors.[21]

One issue that affects all makers of teaching machines, not just learning management systems, is the Family Educational Rights and Privacy Act (FERPA), passed by Congress in 1974, which strictly controls the personally identifiable information that schools can release about students. The government has never been known for catchy acronyms, but it desperately needed Charles Benton's intervention with FERPA (pronounced "fur-pa").

Recall that Encyclopaedia Britannica president Benton changed the name of Electrical Research Products Inc. (ERPI) to Encyclopaedia Britannica Films after overhearing a middle-school student pronounce the name as "burpy."[22]

FERPA advises that "generally, schools must have written permission from the parent or eligible student in order to release any information from a student's education record."[23] This requirement has made universities all the more anxious to enclose student work within a password-protected Web site to comply, and learning management systems accomplish this task extraordinarily well. This requirement tends to lock faculty within the LMS, and it discourages them from using potentially better and more innovative tools that exist in the market. A typical LMS has a complete set of usable, but rudimentary, tools for performing the various functions, such as chat, group discussion, and assessment, but they are rarely in the "best of breed" category and usually cater to the lowest common denominator of user needs. The open nature of the Internet has spawned a large group of easily accessible and often free Web applications that instructors could use if they were not locked in to a restrictive LMS.

It seems clear that learning management systems are here to stay, but some help in opening up their "walled garden" mentality may be on the horizon. A consortium of LMS makers have agreed to create an opening for third-party applications to work seamlessly within their systems to expand their capabilities, though still within password-protected walls. Blackboard, Moodle, Sakai, and Canvas have supported an industry-wide effort, called Learning Tools Interoperability (LTI), which provides a "back door" that allows instructors to safely and seamlessly integrate Web applications from other vendors for students to easily access within the LMS.[24]

The Khan Academy

I briefly mentioned the Khan Academy in chapter 1, but to dismiss the work it is doing as simply providing didactic instructional videos would be to miss the potential of what might evolve. With almost 5,000 short video lessons on math, science, history, and other topics—watched 300 million times—it aspires to go beyond simply delivering instruction and offer a more adaptive and reflexive learning environment. The Khan Academy is a nonprofit company with the drive of a Silicon Valley start-up. Its energetic founder Salman Khan has relentlessly pursued his vision to use

Figure 5.2. Khan Academy founder, Salman Khan.
Ronn Seidenglanz / Khan Academy

Internet-based computing to freely provide a world-class education to any-one, anywhere.[25]

Khan, who gave up a lucrative job at a hedge fund to found the Khan Academy, might seem like an unlikely advocate for universal education, but he exudes a sense of passion for making learning more accessible, par-ticularly in mathematics. Now in his late 30s, Khan (figure 5.2) was born in Metairie, Louisiana, a suburb of New Orleans, the son of a pediatrician from Bangladesh and his Indian-born wife. His parents had a traditionally arranged marriage, and Khan enjoyed a very close extended family, which has had a strong effect on his work.[26]

Khan was a bright student in high school, but he was bored by the lock-step pace that forced him to follow the path dictated by his age. At a regional math competition in tenth grade, he met a student from another school who had tested out of algebra II and was taking precalculus. This concept reso-nated with him, but when he asked his school for the option, he was met with this familiar bureaucratic response: "If we let you do it, we'd have to let everyone do it." Khan ultimately prevailed, but the lesson of individual pacing became an important element in his educational approach.

As an engineering student at the notoriously difficult Massachusetts Institute for Technology, he followed this strategy by joining a group known as the class-skippers. Feeling they were wasting their time passively sitting in 300-person lectures taught by professors giving the same boring lecture for the hundredth time, the class-skippers used the time they would have spent in class to actively engage with the material using a textbook or online resources. Some of these students were able to take twice as many highly challenging engineering classes per semester and still received high grades. This group included Khan's friend Shantanu Sinha, the high schooler who had tested out of algebra II; Shantanu would ultimately become the Khan Academy's president.[27]

Khan and Shantanu returned to MIT after graduation and used their class-skipping technique to earn multiple graduate degrees. Khan went to Silicon Valley to begin his career working at a number of Internet startups, but he returned to Cambridge to study for an MBA at Harvard, after determining that "Silicon Valley in the late 1990s was the absolute worst place to find a wife or girlfriend." Khan did indeed meet his future wife, a Harvard medical student, who now practices in Mountain View.[28]

Teaching Nadia

While at a family wedding in 2004, Khan chatted with his 12-year-old cousin Nadia, who was struggling with math. Nadia was a straight-A student in her New Orleans prep school, but she had done poorly on a placement exam that would set her future academic path. It was clear to Khan that Nadia was bright and motivated, and he offered to tutor her remotely from Boston. They used the telephone and a drawing program from Yahoo that allowed them to draw freehand on the same virtual screen, some 1,500 miles apart.[29]

Those tutoring sessions provided a working laboratory for Khan to work out some of the ideas that would ultimately form his now-famous video lessons. Noticing that Nadia sometimes would guess at the answers, he made it clear to her that it was okay for her to say that she didn't understand an idea and needed some guidance.[30]

Nadia retook her math placement exam and of course passed with flying colors. By 2006, Khan was tutoring other family members, but he found the logistics of scheduling the synchronous phone meetings difficult. A friend suggested he use Google's new video-sharing service, YouTube, to host his videos. At the time YouTube limited the length of videos to only 10 minutes, but this turned out to be the ideal length for learning, as later suggested by cognitive researchers. He wrote some simple math quizzing software, and the foundation for the Khan Academy was established.[31]

Khan worried that the process of making videos would become more like movie-making than tutoring, saying, "Tutoring is intimate. You talk with someone, not at them." He was concerned that showing his face might distract from the teaching process and chose to act like the wizard of Oz, hidden behind the curtain,[32] with only his rough drawing slowly emerging on the screen as he spoke.[33] His videos became very popular because of YouTube's ease of discovery and vast audience.

Khan was working full time at a hedge fund while creating hundreds of videos from a closet in his home. In 2009, he decided to quit his day job and pursue the Khan Academy full time, relying primarily on small donations. One day he received a $10,000 check from Ann Doerr, wife of the highly successful venture capitalist, John Doerr, who recalled, "I decided I wanted to send a little contribution . . . Then I found out I was his biggest contributor. The other thing I found out that he was about ready to call it a day and get a 'real' job, which was to me equally frightening."[34]

Around the same time, Microsoft founder and recent education philanthropist Bill Gates mentioned Khan's videos while speaking at the prestigious Aspen Ideas Conference, saying that he was using Khan's videos with his own kids and that Salman Kahn was his favorite teacher. Shortly thereafter, the Bill and Melinda Gates Foundation, Google, Ann and John Doerr, and several other foundations got together to provide millions of dollars of funding to start Khan Academy. The academy is an incredibly media savvy company when compared with typical nonprofits. Perhaps it is this combination of high technology and Silicon Valley backers that has fostered the almost unbelievable hagiography of the Khan creation story, but it is gaining acceptance by a wide range of learners, including homeschoolers, public school students, and adult learners.[35]

Mathematics at the Khan Academy

Of all Khan Academy's curricular content areas, basic mathematics is the most complete. I spent some time on the mathematics section and

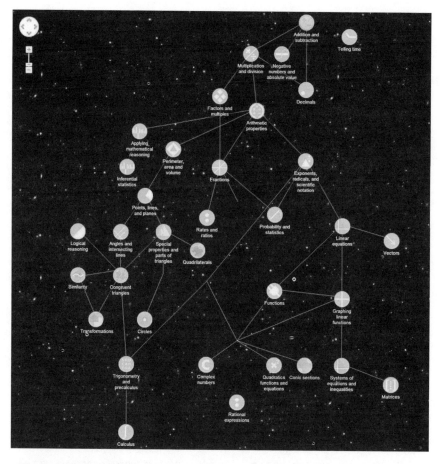

Figure 5.3. Khan Academy's mathematics content knowledge map.
Khan Academy

found the site well organized and potentially useful. The basic pedagogical model is to have the student take a pretest on current understandings, then create a suggested series of topics to learn based on a content model of the overall subject area (figure 5.3).

Like an intelligent tutoring system, the Web site creates a rudimentary student model of what a learner knows and does not yet know. This model is used to help guide the learner as what to study next. The student model is always visible to the student (and the teacher, if the student is part of a class), both to provide both guidance and encouragement. The student is

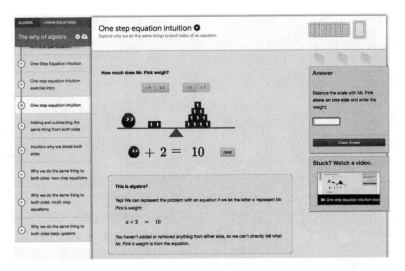

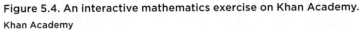

Figure 5.4. An interactive mathematics exercise on Khan Academy.
Khan Academy

presented with a series of questions on a given concept (figure 5.4) and is given immediate feedback to his questions.

Students are offered an unlimited number of tries, but they must answer five questions in a row correctly before moving on to the next concept. I found this a little tedious, particularly after missing the fifth one for a careless error and having to start the process over again. When stuck, students can ask for up to five hints per concept and can also view a video covering the topic.

There is no error diagnosis as to why answers were incorrect, so the same instruction and examples are offered for both initial instruction and remediation. ITS developer Peter Brusilovsky predicted that the massive amounts of data collected by the millions of problems completed by students each day, coupled with the academy's generous funding, might provide critical mass toward offering a more personalized learning experience in the future.[36]

As well implemented as the Khan Academy software is, and as rosy its future might be, not everyone agrees that Khan's approach is moving educational technology forward. Serious games developer Marc Prensky is critical about Khan's superficial application of gamification in the Web site, evidenced by learners earning points and digital "badges" to encourage their progress. He also echoes critics, including constructivist Logo advocates, who claim Khan is doing "old things in new ways" by providing simple didactic lectures and drill and practice, where more thoughtful exploratory methods might help develop the kind of thinking skills that 21st-century citizens will need.[37]

Computer Science at the Khan Academy

From the days of intelligent tutoring systems, computer programming has been a popular target for computer-based educational efforts, and the Khan Academy has developed a robust and highly interactive Introduction to Programming course written by John Resiq, Khan's dean of computer science and a legendary figure among JavaScript* programmers. At age 22, Resiq wrote jQuery, a JavaScript library used by almost all advanced JavaScript sites.

Resiq was inspired by some innovative work by Bret Victor, a former interface designer for Apple, who has advocated for a more dynamic approach to computer programming. In response to the question, how do we get people to understand programming? Victor responds, "We change programming. We turn it into something that's understandable by people."[38] In traditional computer science classes, students are taught the building blocks and then apply them to writing programs. They submit their programs to the computer to run. If they need to change anything, they must perform the edit-submit-see cycle all over again. Victor insists this is not the best way to teach programming, and a more direct connection is needed between the program and what it actually does.

In some ways, the process of programming a computer hasn't changed much from the days when people wrote programs on punch cards and submitted them to a white lab-coated technician sitting behind a glass window. He would run your program on the computer and return a paper printout hours, or even days, later. Over time, interactive terminals and personal computers eliminated the need to use punch cards in favor of a form of word processing, but the process is still as indirect. The programmer types out lines of code on a text editor, submits them to the computer to run, and then evaluates the results.

*JavaScript is a popular computer language used to develop Web-based applications.

Figure 5.5. Responsive programming environment.
Courtesy Bret Victor, worrydream.com

Victor's approach is to make the process of programming instant and direct. Programmers still write programs in a text editor, but the computer instantly reflects the results of any changes made. If the program's goal is to draw a tree and sun and you change the code controlling the color, the result would be visually apparent the instant you changed the number representing the color (figure 5.5).[39]

The Khan Academy's programming course uses a tool similar to the one Victor built. You type code on one side of the screen and instantly see the results on the other. But there are some interesting twists. Rather than using videos for primary instruction, as in the other Khan courses, the site makes use of what it calls *code talk-throughs.*

In a talk-through, a disembodied voice narrates as code is typed on the screen, and the output emerges in real-time. At any point, learners can pause the playback and begin changing the code themselves to explore what might happen when modifying what the instructor did, and the results appear instantly. They've added sophisticated error-catching capabilities and make adding predefined code elements very easy to do. They have also included features to encourage a way of programming that modern programmers use to explore new areas, such as "worked examples" of small programs, and they have incorporated tools that mimic the popular knowledge-sharing site Stack Overflow and source-code-sharing tool GitHub.

Bret Victor has raised some questions about the Khan Academy's incarnation of his responsive programming tool, maintaining that providing live coding and talk-throughs is a good start but not enough to teach programming properly; channeling Seymour Papert, he feels that a good programming tool "must support and encourage powerful ways of thinking and enable programmers to see and understand the execution of their programs."[40] As a programmer and someone who has tried to teach many people to program, I have to agree with him. Getting people to understand programmatic thinking is much harder than simplifying the syntax, and like other critics of the math programs, I worry that this, too, is old content in new clothing. That said, it's a solid base to build on, and I'll be interested to see how it may evolve in the future.

MOOCs and MOOCs

If one is to believe the press, from obscure educational journals to the *New York Times*, the teaching machine for the start of twenty-first century is the massive open online course. There are those who view MOOCs as the savior to managing the ever-spiraling cost of higher education, and others who see them as sowing the seeds of the demise of the university as we know it. The truth, of course, lies somewhere between. Discussing technologies that are still evolving can be a bit tricky. As I write this, most of the MOOC providers are less than two years old and are in a constant state of change, but some emerging patterns are worth exploring.

Working backward through the acronym, MOOCs are *courses* taught *online*. They are asynchronous but typically have a defined start and end time and cover a specific topic and use the Internet to deliver curricular content that the learner can consume. Assessments are given, sometimes within the video-based content, sometimes summatively, and sometimes there are problems to be solved. MOOCs are *open* to anyone to take, typically at no cost, and can involve a *massive* number of simultaneous learners, often thousands at a time.

MOOCs burst onto higher education in full force in 2012, fueled by large amounts of Silicon Valley–based venture capital and publicity in the popular press, but they had a namesake some five years earlier in Canada. Canadian MOOCs shared the same four-letter acronym and their use of the Internet, but not much more. As different as the Canadian MOOCs are from their eponymous Silicon Valley MOOCs, both are important teaching machines to examine.

Canadian MOOCS

In 2000, the educator and information theorist George Siemens was using educational technology such as blogs and wikis to engage students in his teaching at Winnipeg's Red Deer College, but he found a deaf ear from his colleagues when it came to adopting these participatory tools in their own classrooms. Siemens began blogging about his experiences with these new tools, and he was able to connect with like-minded educators across Canada and the world. Together, they formed a "personal learning network" of educators and technologists who saw the value in a more participatory pedagogy, and the potential power of the new Internet-driven technology to facilitate learning. Their discussions helped them articulate a theoretical framework Siemens named *connectivism*.[41]

Connectivism emerged from research in the cognitive sciences and social psychology, and it emphasizes the external and social components of learning in the Internet age. In connectivism, the assumption is that knowledge is networked and distributed in the world, and the act of knowing is found by being connected with that networked information in personal and meaningful ways. Learning occurs in a complicated and chaotic manner by forming new connections with these networks, our own internal neural and conceptual networks, and other people's internal networks. Connectivists believe that this process can be enhanced by using technology, in particular, the communicative power of the Internet.[42]

In 2008, Siemens, now at the University of Manitoba, approached one of the members of his network, New Brunswick researcher Stephen Downes, to co-facilitate a new kind of course that used the ideas and technology of connectivism to teach the concepts of connectivism. Connectivism and Connective Knowledge (CCK08) would "be distributed in the environment" using resources from the Internet that were linked to, rather than confined behind a learning management system like typical e-learning courses. CCK08 was to be learner-driven, with the "instructors" serving as facilitators and the learners themselves contributing to course design and resources used.[43]

Siemens and Downes approached another member of their network, educational technologist Dave Cormier from the University of Prince Edwards Island, to participate and design the technical infrastructure for the new course. Cormier had been interested in educational technology since teaching English in Korea in 2001, and he was convinced of technology's ability to facilitate the learning process for the 270 students in his classes. Cormier was fascinated with the social construction element of the learning process, and he viewed technology as a mechanism to navigate this new landscape of knowledge that networked technology had transformed from a world of scarcity into a world of abundance.[44]

CCK08 was offered by the University of Manitoba in the fall of 2008, initially with 25 credit-receiving, tuition-paying students, but in the spirit of open access, the facilitators decided that anyone could participate, since it was taught completely online. The course quickly became an experiment in scale, with 2,400 people ultimately participating. Only the initial 25 students received college credit for the course, but a new educational genre was being introduced.[45] During a Skype chat conversation with Siemens about what to call this new pedagogical structure, Cormier proposed the acronym MOOC, and higher education had a new instructional category,[46] only to be adopted five years later by groups who had very different ideas of what the name represented.

Over the years, dozens of connectivist MOOCs have been facilitated using a wide range of technologies, including email, Facebook, RSS, blogs, wikis, WordPress, Drupal, Twitter, and Moodle. But the formula typically contains many of the same elements: learn control over the interactive process, offer weekly synchronous meetings with the facilitators and guest speakers, and provide a weekly email newsletter summarizing the activity in the social media used. These courses emphasize learner autonomy and the use of social media to self-organize and make sense of complex subject areas and aim at expanding learners' abilities to share their understandings with the class by creating digital artifacts, such as blogs, videos, images, and concept maps.[47]

The originators of the Canadian MOOCs are hopeful that even though the Silicon Valley MOOCs do not embrace the connectivist philosophy, and the tools do not promote the same level of participatory learning as their more connectivist approach would like, their learners are indeed finding ways to authentically connect with each other, though the MOOCs were not designed to facilitate this. Stephen Downes once commented, "Life finds a way," alluding to a line from Ian Malcolm, the chaotician in *Jurassic Park*, uses in explaining how the park's dinosaurs have begun to breed in spite of a formalized system the park's designers put in place to prevent them from doing so.[48]

California MOOCs

As innovative and revolutionary as the connectivist MOOCs were, they did not capture the attention of the media and higher education in quite the same way that the current generation of e-learning companies that have adopted the MOOC moniker have done. If the Canadian MOOCs drew inspiration from John Dewey and Seymour Papert's learner-centered approaches, the new MOOCs have followed a more didactic, content-centric, and instructor-driven process. They provide a specific set of content for a course of study and instruction using short video clips to deliver intimate but one-directional tutoring over the Internet.

Learners are given an opportunity to test their understandings through quizzes and other assessments, often directly embedded within the video clips. Some more progressive providers offer interactive environments, such as simulations and test beds, both to instruct and to assess understandings. Homework is assigned and graded using a variety of automated methods, and an overall grade for the course is given at the end.

The modern MOOC era began on October 10, 2011, when Stanford computer science professor Sebastian Thrun and Google's director of research, Peter Norvig, offered CS221, Introduction to Computer Science, to over 160,000 registered learners, resulting in what some have termed, "the online Woodstock of the digital era."[49] The graduate-level class was taught simultaneously in person at Stanford and through video over the Web. Over 200 students came to the first class, but attendance quickly dwindled to about 30 when the students evidently preferred to watch the YouTube videos rather than come to class. In the end, over 20,000 students completed the course, receiving a "statement of accomplishment" but no Stanford credits.[50]

Sebastian Thrun (figure 5.6) is a man who is not afraid of taking on big projects. Channeling his mentor, Google founder Larry Page, he remarked, "If you don't think big, you don't do big things. Whether it's a big problem

Figure 5.6. Udacity founder Sebastian Thrun.
Udacity

or a small problem, I spend the same amount of time on it—so I might as well take a big problem that really moves society forward." The German-born Thrun studied computer science statistics at the University of Bonn and in 1995 came to Carnegie Mellon University, where he developed a passion for robotics.[51]

After a sabbatical year spent at Stanford in 2001, Thrun was bitten by the Silicon Valley spirit and joined the Stanford computer science faculty. He took a year off from Stanford in 2007 to work with Google, where he founded Google X, a successful skunk works* that developed Google's Streetview

---

*A *skunk works* is a small group within a larger organization that is given a high degree of autonomy to develop new project, unhampered by the typical bureaucracy.

360-degree image-mapping feature in Google Maps and the new Google Glass augmented-reality glasses.[52]

Like many of the new MOOC developers, he credits Salman Khan as the inspiration behind his foray into online education. After giving a TED talk in March 2011 to evangelize the self-driving cars he was developing at Google, Thrun saw Khan take the stage and speak passionately about his "one world classroom" concept, joined by Bill Gates, who called Khan's efforts "the future of education."[53] Thrun had done some thinking a few years before about e-learning; and while he liked the idea of MIT's OpenCourseWare, he found it too rigid, and overly based on long classroom lectures.

Khan's more intimate direct instructional approach struck a chord with him, and two months later he formed a company using $300,000 of his own money.[54] Instead of the proverbial Silicon Valley garage, KnowLabs was born in the guest house at his home near Stanford where he had developed the CS221 class. When enrollment passed 100,000 students, Strum knew they were onto something, and with an infusion of venture capital, KnowLabs transformed into Udacity to pursue the idea.[55]

Unlike most of the other MOOC developers, who want to work in cooperation with existing institutions of higher education, Thrun sees them as a system in need of disruption. "Fifty years from now, there will be only 10 institutions in the world that deliver higher education," he predicts, and he hopes that Udacity will be one of them. The company foresees a variety of potential revenue opportunities, such as charging learners for help from teaching assistants, credentialing, and providing a recruitment service identifying their strongest students for industry.

Udacity operates more like a Hollywood studio than a university. Faculty are paid $5,000 to $10,000 to teach a course, while professional video crews create the instructional video clips. Like the elite university they sprang from, Udacity's programming staff is very selective about those they choose as instructors, rejecting 98 percent who ask to teach classes. A company executive looks forward to the day when teachers "are compensated like a TV actor or movie actor" because "students want to learn from the best teacher."[56]

Thrun was not the only computer science professor at Stanford who was impressed by the massive interest in the CS221 class. Computer science professor Andrew Ng usually taught a course in machine learning to a classroom of typically 400 students at Stanford. In the fall of 2011, he took

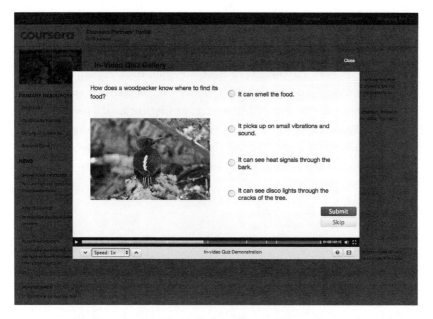

Figure 5.7. A quiz embedded in a Coursera video clip.
Coursera

that class online, using video clips to connect with an audience of over 100,000 students, and has not looked back. "To reach that many students before," Ng said, "I would have had to teach my normal Stanford class for 250 years."[57]

Ng and his colleague Daphne Koller saw an opportunity in education and formed Coursera in 2012, with the help of $65 million in venture capital. So far, they are the largest of the MOOC providers, with some 83 partner institutions (including my own, the University of Virginia) providing 431 courses to 4.5 million learners as of 2013.[58] Coursera has taken higher education by storm and sent universities scrambling to offer Coursera courses. In stark contrast to the Canadian MOOCs, both Udacity and Coursera have built highly centralized LMS-like software to deliver annotated video lectures, punctuated by periodic quizzes, following a more didactic pedagogical model.

Coursera is not trying to disrupt higher education by developing an alternative learning institution as Udacity is doing, but it is likely to be as equally disruptive from within. Coursera partners with universities to deliver courses through its online platform, and while the company provides guidance, the schools own the courses and are solely responsible for their content and production.[59]

Because of their partnership business model, the company has a very different revenue opportunity than Udacity. Agreements involve a revenue sharing arrangement with the partner institutions. The details are still evolving, but options include a publishing model for courses, such as textbook publishers currently use, charging for university course credits (sometimes called "pay for paper"), and fees for anti-cheating verification and proctored testing.[60]

Ivy League MOOCs

The area surrounding Boston known as Route 128 was a powerhouse for innovation in the 1960s and 1970s, dotted with companies that shaped the computer industry, such as BBN Technologies, Wang, Digital Equipment Corporation (DEC), Data General, and Apollo. As if to lay claim to their innovation heritage, Harvard and MIT have joined forces to provide a MOOC platform called edX that has some potential to be a player in this fast-evolving educational landscape. Because it is nonprofit and open source, edX stands in a sharp counterpoint to the more commercial ventures of Udacity and Coursera.

Anant Agarwal has been steeped in entrepreneurial spirit since he was 12 years old, running a small egg business in his native India. He went on to found several innovative microprocessor companies while working as a professor at MIT's Department of Computer Science and Engineering and winning numerous awards for his teaching. In spite of being a gifted teacher, Agarwal recognized the potential of computer-meditated educational tools accessed via the Internet, saying, "Great lectures make for good theater, but the future of education is online."[61]

In late 2011, MIT formed a venture called MITx, to explore delivering its courses online and asked Agarwal to direct the effort. MIT has a rich history of providing back-of-the-classroom lectures and resources with the university's OpenCourseWare project, but it was looking for a more comprehensive learning environment that went beyond the unidirectional broadcast model and might conceivably exceed, not just equal, the in-person classroom experience. In another example of the impact that Salman Khan's videos have had on online education, Agarwal credits Khan for opening his eyes to using

Figure 5.8. Creating a video clip for an edX course.
edX

video saying, "He was my student [at MIT] and an inspiration for the MOOC movement." But Agarwal wanted to "move beyond providing content on the Web to the 3Cs—course, community, and certificate!"[62]

MITx chose to create an online version of a 6.002, Circuits and Electronics, a required, sophomore-level engineering class, as its initial offering. Circuits and Electronics was a demanding course in electronic circuit design that made heavy use of in-person laboratory time. Agarwal and his team developed a series of innovative online simulations of the lab experiments to replace the in-person laboratory experience with active learning components. They recorded a series of short video instructional clips, which were interspersed with quizzes, interactive tutorials, and videos of functioning circuits (figure 5.8).

The course debuted in the 2012 spring semester, open to anyone, with four teaching assistants (TAs) providing support to the learners. The TAs tried to provide answers to questions as they came in, but they were completely overwhelmed by the 154,763 learners who ultimately registered. The majority of these people was casually checking out the site and had no intention of taking the class; but 25,750 students were considered serious students, and 7,157 completed it, earning a certificate.[63]

To cope with these huge numbers of questions, Agarwal advised his TAs to delay answering for a couple of hours and let students work through problems on their own or let other students help each other in the discussion forums. MITx put in place a system of "voting up" student responses to other student questions, something akin to Facebook's "Like" option. Answerers received "karma points" when enough students believed the answerer had truly helped the student's question, and the points gave them more privileges. In the end, students waited only an average of 47 minutes before their questions were finally answered.[64]

Buoyed by the results, MIT met with Harvard University and decided to work together to develop a platform for providing quality online education. They formed the nonprofit venture edX with a $60 million joint investment, made up from institutional support, philanthropy, other universities, and grants. Stressing the emphasis on quality, MIT's Provost L. Rafael Reif stated, "This is not to be construed as MIT-lite, or Harvard-lite. The content is the same content" as the residential classes.[65] There has been a groundswell of interest from other educational institutions to join Harvard and MIT. Initially, the University of California at Berkeley and Georgetown University joined edX, and the number of prestigious partners continues to grow, including Boston University, the California Institute of Technology, Cornell, Davidson, Karolinska Institutet, McGill, Rice, University of Texas, Wellesley, and others.[66]

Even though edX is a nonprofit venture, it was not designed to be a loss for MIT, Harvard, and the other partnering institutions, and it will begin charging students for activities such as certification and exam proctoring. Like Coursera, edX views its financial relationship with academic partners as a true partnership, where any potential revenues are shared. It is are also exploring the possibility of offering the platform to corporations and NGOs, such as the International Monetary Fund, and hopes to break even in the next three years.[67]

The Potential Side Effects of Venture Capital

One of the more concerning issues about Coursera and Udacity is the source of their funding, venture capitalists. Venture capital is provided by investment firms to fund early stage companies. These firms typically invest in a large number of startups with the assumption that 90 percent of them will fail, but the 10 percent that thrive will yield a return on investment of at least 300 percent (known as a "3-bagger"). This strategy has been extremely successful in the high-technology sector and in large part is responsible for the phenomenal products and companies that have emerged from Silicon Valley. Venture capital firms provide a strong support network to help guide new entrepreneurs, but their model has its darker side.

There is an inherent instability in any "disposable" relationship. The funded companies typically cede a significant amount of control in exchange for the millions of dollars they receive. When the company delivers the kinds of profits that the funders see as significant, that control can be very constructive and nurturing. But if the company underperforms or takes longer to deliver, it can find itself among the "walking dead," with just enough capital to stay in business but not enough to grow, closed down completely, or merged with another of the firm's portfolio of funded companies.[68]

Education has been a notoriously difficult environment to thrive in financially in and slow to adopt change. The question will be how patient the funders of Coursera and Udacity will be if growth does not develop rapidly enough relative to their other potential revenue opportunities. Sebastian Thrun and Daphne Koller may be ideologically driven to make a difference in education, but it's not clear how long their backers will support them if they can't produce significant financial returns.

Scaling the Grading and Feedback Process

Providing fast, individualized feedback to students on assigned work is one of the biggest problems for all distance-learning programs, from correspondence schools to MOOCs. The Chautauquas provided this feedback by organizing groups that met locally when possible; if not, they sent written feedback through the postal system. The International Correspondence Schools employed a legion of employees tasked with rapidly grading student work and mailing it back, which often took weeks. Modern for-profit e-learning universities have a quicker mechanism via the Internet, but the burden of correcting papers and answering questions is done on a one-to-one basis that is not easily scaled. MOOCs have an even tougher problem to solve. The number of students participating makes individual attention a physical and financial impossibility, and this very high level of participation will continue for as long as most MOOCs are provided for free, or at a very reduced cost.

Some academic subjects have deterministic answers to problems that present easy responses, such as numbers or symbols that are easily understood by a computer. Mathematics and computer programming lend themselves to various forms of automated grading systems, as we saw in the Khan Academy and early ITS efforts to teach the Lisp programming language. The difficulty comes when trying to assess more humanistic student responses, such as writing, and answers to higher-order thinking problems that are not as easily scored by machine. It is possible to evaluate these responses using well-constructed multiple-choice assessments, which computers can score easily, but some MOOC providers are experimenting with some more innovative solutions to solve this thorny problem.

Coursera uses a variation of a technique known as calibrated peer review (CPR), which enables students to grade each other's work in a systematic and fair manner. CPR was initially developed by UCLA chemistry professor Orville Chapman in the late 1990s, under a grant from the National Science Foundation, to help relieve chemistry instructors from the burden of hand-correcting written homework assignments, and it has been successfully used in many other disciplines.

In the beginning, the instructor assigns the students to rate three sample responses to the same assignment using a rubric.* Each student is then given a *credibility weighting* number, which measures the extent to which their assessments agree with an instructor's grading of the same responses. When the instructor assigns a problem and the students turn in their assignments online, they then anonymously score three of their fellow students' responses to the assignment, as well as their own response using the same rubric. As a result of this activity, each student's assignment is graded four times, and the scores are weighted by the rater's credibility rating to yield the final grade (figure 5.9).[69]

Another solution to scaling the assessment of student writing responses is automatic essay scoring (AES). AES is a technique developed by compu-

*A *rubric* is a set of questions a grader uses to assign a score to an assignment, such as "Did the student mention electricity in the answer?" In CPR, each question is graded from 1–6 and added together to come up with the total score.

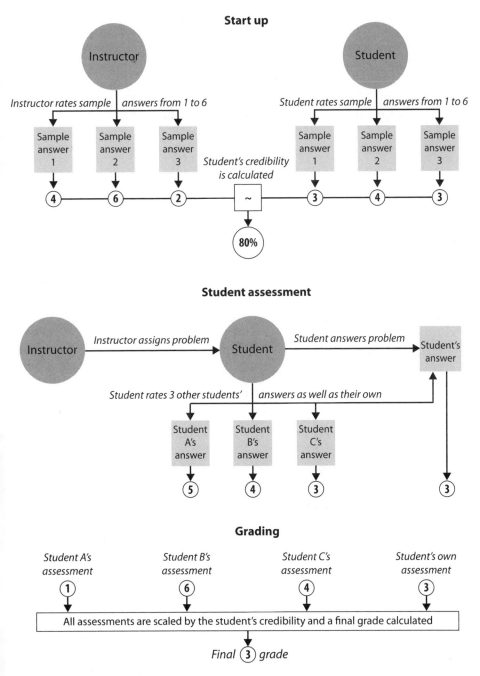

Figure 5.9. Calibrated peer review.

tational linguists to automatically grade student writing by comparing it with hundreds of other essays on the same topic that have been scored by human scorers and then returning the likely score that essay may yield when graded by a teacher. More sophisticated AES systems can offer the student precise feedback about how to improve the essay.

Ellis Page pioneered automated essay scoring in the mid-1960s with his Project Essay Grader (PEG) software. PEG applied statistical techniques such as multiple linear regression to essays, and he considered such factors as essay length, number of commas, prepositions, and uncommon words in a weighted model of what he thought approximated the internal structures used by human raters. Page found a very high correlation between his PEG system results and human raters of the same essays.[70]

The next 30 years led to vigorous research into the automatic scoring of essays using a wide range of mathematical techniques and factors within the essays, including Bayesian inference, latent semantic analysis, and neural networks. The overall manner in which they work is similar. Typically, human raters hand-score hundreds of sample essays reflecting the full range of possible quality levels. This scoring is put through rigorous inter-rater reliability testing to ensure the accuracy of the human ratings. The essays, with the ratings, are entered into the AES system to train it on the essay topic. Once trained, the system, in a matter of seconds develops an internal model of what an arbitrary essay written on the same topic might score.[71]

The Educational Testing Service (ETS), which administers the SAT and other tests, began experimenting in the 1990s with natural-language-processing and information retrieval techniques to provide automated scoring of essays. They tested their system using the analytical writing assessment portion contained in the Graduate Management Admissions Test (GMAT), used for admission to MBA programs. Their e-rater system used linear regression of over 100 essay features to provide a high degree of agreement with human raters. The ETS e-rater system yielded an 87–94 percent agreement with human-scored essays. (These correlations are comparable with those researchers would expect among essays scored by two or more human scorers.) Based on these results, ETS eventually abandoned the use of human readers for the GMAT in favor of automated essay scoring.[72]

Most AES software has been proprietary and expensive, but edX has added an automated essay scoring capability to its e-learning platform that allows automated grading of short, student-written responses. Instructors need to hand-grade 100 essays first and then the system will automatically grade any number of essays beyond that. But not everybody believes in AES's ability to provide meaningful assessment of such a human product. A group called the Professionals against Machine Scoring of Student Essays in High-Stakes Assessment, which includes the linguist and activist Noam Chomsky, countered, "Let's face the realities of automatic essay scoring. Computers cannot 'read.' They cannot measure the essentials of effective written communication: accuracy, reasoning, adequacy of evidence, good sense, ethical stance, convincing argument, meaningful organization, clarity, and veracity, among others."[73]

Calibrated peer review and automated essay scoring are just the beginning of the movement to scale up the grading of student work. The sheer numbers of MOOC participants, coupled with these systems' ability to record all of a student's actions while online with the provider, will provide a significant amount of raw data for machine learning and other data-mining techniques to tease assessments of what learners know and still need to understand. It will be interesting to see what evolves.

Big Data

Big data is a phrase used in the popular press to describe the collection of large amounts of information that can be later analyzed to find specific trends and correlations. Marketers, Google, Amazon, Netflix, and, of course, the National Security Administration use data-mining techniques that are able to piece together far-flung morsels of data and weave a larger story by comparing it with other patterns. Amazon's book recommendations are good examples of mining big data from a number of small actions. As you browse their site, Amazon collects all the places you have gone, reviews you have read, things you have bought, and so forth. This information is compared to the way other people do those things, and correlations are then mathematically teased out of the huge collection of little facts to suggest that if you browsed for *East of Eden*, you might enjoy *The Great Gatsby* or *The Catcher in the Rye*.[74]

Using big data is not a new idea of the Internet age. In the days when the best way to target advertising directly to a person was through the U.S. Postal Service, direct mailers used a technique known as *offer testing* or *A/B testing* to see what impact changing small things in the mailing would have on the response rate. Because they mailed to thousands of people at a time, they had a perfect test bed for seeing the effect of changes. These marketers would change some factor, such as the price, wording, even the color of the type for a small percentage of the mailing and compare that response with the response from the standard version.[75] Amazon, Google, and a host of other Internet companies are continually publishing changes to their Web sites to test an almost infinite number of possibilities before releasing them to their full audience.[76]

Salman Khan decided early on in his videos that showing his face would not be as productive as simply showing him drawing on the screen, but that was just his personal hunch. Coursera is using A/B testing to empirically evaluate a wide variety of ways the presenter can appear (e.g., over the shoulder, screen only, small video inset, etc.). Coursera can change the method of presentation for a subset of its learners and then compare the results of the various permutations, and they will be able to back their early guesses with hard data.[77]

The traditional classroom is a difficult place for true experimentation. There are too few students to employ the powerful statistical techniques used in medicine and the hard sciences. In the future, A/B testing, coupled with the large number of learners that the MOOCs amass may create an ideal experimental laboratory for evaluating the effectiveness of a wide variety of techniques beyond the size of the video, for obtaining empirical evidence for different pedagogical methods, and for gaining insight into how people learn.

Both Coursera and Udacity see a big opportunity in collecting and analyzing the minute details of student behavior. Daphne Koller believes that it "opens new avenues for understanding learning," exposing the hidden pathways learners use to plot their way through the learning process. Strun predicts that we have seen only the "the tip of the iceberg," and the massive quantities of data are perfect for computer analysis; each student action, "no matter how inconsequential it may seem, becomes grist for the statistical mill."[78]

Making Sense of Cloud Learning

It is hard to look at all these new networked applications and not be sanguine about their potential, but the same was said about prior technological efforts. It is still too early to judge their impact. Many of the same philosophical, political, and pedagogical issues remain contentious, but never before have we been able to scale the availability to so many people for such a low incremental cost.

As critical as some people are about the for-profit e-learning systems, they fulfill a real need for many learners. Like the correspondence schools, they provide a service for people who may be unable to attend more traditional institutions, and they also offer much-needed credentialing. Using Internet technology enables them to bridge geographic barriers, but pedagogically they perpetuate the traditional didactic classroom and ultimately suffer from William Bowden's cost-disease model of not being able to scale as productively as some of the other Internet-based providers.[79]

The learning management system provides an appealing way for instructors and institutions to manage Internet-based learning materials, as evidenced by their near 100 percent adoption in colleges and universities. Like trees restricting the forest's underbrush, however, LMSs have dramatically inhibited the development of alternative technologies that may not impose the same content-driven pedagogy. The recent move to support third-party plug-in applications through LTI is a promising break from the LMS hegemony.

The Khan Academy embraces many of the basic principles of earlier teaching machines, even though the pedagogical model still clings to didactic explanations in the videos bolstered by drill and practice, particularly in the mathematics section. Students proceed at their own pace through the curricular content and must they demonstrate masterly level learning in order to move on to the next concept. They receive instant feedback on their assessments, and they can request automated hints and remedial instruction.

The Khan computer science curriculum has a nice mixture of didactic explanation and constructivist exploration because of its ability to instantly experiment and run code fragments during the code talk-throughs. The beginnings of ITS-style content and student models hint at a more sophisticated direction toward making truly individual and effective pathways to learning. Finally, the Khan Academy's commitment to data mining the massive amounts of student activity records could yield a potentially powerful environment for empirically testing educational strategies and techniques.

MOOCs are currently an experiment in quantity, not quality. As Clay Shirky observed, "The effect of MOOCs on the academy, though, is no more likely to be about pedagogy than the effect of MP3s on the music industry was about audio quality. The adoption of nontraditional forms of education hinges on accessibility, flexibility, and cost—not quality."[80] They are currently providing very much the same kind of experience as a large audience classroom lecture broken down into smaller chunks and an online quiz tossed in every now and then.

To view MOOCs in their present form is probably not a good prediction of how they might evolve. But with classes filled with thousands of students and activity data being collected to the level of a mouse click, they are a potential laboratory for educational research on a scale we have never seen before. The ability to subtly change factors for subgroups of learners and measure the results of those changes offers an unprecedented ability to experimentally test all kinds of new learning strategies.

6

Making Sense of Teaching Machines

After examining more than a century of innovators using the technology of their time to enable people to learn differently than they did in the traditional didactic classroom, it is clear that the goals of these efforts were often different. The Chautauquas, correspondence schools, and e-learning sought to solve a geographic problem to free learners from having to attend classes in person. Instructional radio and television, as well as the massive open online courses, hoped to achieve economies of scale by leveraging a broadcast model to large audiences, both in real time and asynchronously. Programmed instruction and Logo were ideologically driven by theorists who believed they had discovered important new insights into how people learn. PLATO and the intelligent tutoring systems looked to harness the computer as the ultimate teaching machine.

By looking at the group through a common set of lenses, a number of themes emerge, despite their different motivations and the technologies the individual efforts employed. Regardless of their pedagogical foundation, many adopted individual pacing, rapid feedback, and mastery learning. These pedagogical methods seem to surface and emerge naturally, perhaps as a response to some basic issues in technology-moderated education, and warrant our attention.

The ability to achieve higher economies of scale is often the sole raison d'être for forays into educational technology, and it has been a critical motivator for almost all the teaching machines examined here. One-on-one tutoring may be the gold standard in terms of effective instruction, yielding the highest academic return of any pedagogical method,[1] but it is too expensive to practically implement on a wide basis.

No place is more political than the field of education, the K–12 classroom in particular. The issues surrounding the public funding of education, equity, accreditation, teacher's unions, and overall maintenance of the status quo of educational institutions greatly affect how new innovations are viewed, as innovations may threaten one or more of those sensitive issues. Politics is also typically intertwined deeply with economic issues that technological interventions usually raise.

The "better mousetrap theory" has not been a particularly effective model for encouraging the adoption of any technological innovation, and education is no exception. The *diffusion of innovations* research provides a good framework for understanding how teaching machines were presented and adopted by their constituencies and what they might have done to increase their odds of success.[2]

Pedagogical Methods
Teaching machines are reflections of the basic pedagogical models their developers fundamentally preferred. The correspondence schools, radio, television, e-learning, and the non-Canadian MOOCs tended to follow the more didactic, instructor-centered pedagogy found in traditional classroom instruction. The instructor, whether in person, in text, or on video, takes the role of an all-knowing deliverer of curricular content to the learner. The student's job is to consume, understand, and remember that content.

The mechanical machines of Sidney Pressey and B. F. Skinner, programmed instruction books, the PLATO system, and CD-ROM-based games followed the theoretical leanings of behavioral psychology. Pedagogy based on this framework can be very successful in some content areas if learning goals have been analyzed properly. Curricular content can then be divided into a series of small stimulus-response interactions, and the learner's behavior can be shaped by rewarding correct responses. Learning emerges from a large number of these small steps designed to lead toward mastery of the content.

Seymour Papert's Logo movement forged its way under the banner of constructionism, in which students learned by direct experience with microworlds that created a simplified environment for exploring abstract problems in a very tangible manner. Papert took guidance from Jean Piaget's theory of constructivism, in which Piaget conceived of children building understandings of their worlds without the need for formal teaching. Education came from the bottom up, rather than the top down, and the students learned through personal discovery and the ability to connect new ideas with those previously held concepts. The serious games movement took cues from both Piaget and Papert and offered new microworlds for exploration, but with elements of entertainment to encourage more engagement from the learners.

The Canadian MOOCs subscribed to the connectivist pedagogical model, which also applied some of the ideas explored by Piaget and Papert to the networked world enabled by the Internet. Knowledge is distributed throughout that world, and learners can make their own meaning in personal and meaningful ways by forming new connections with these networks and their own internal neural and conceptual networks.

There are, of course, many cases where the boundary lines cannot be drawn so sharply. The Khan Academy straddles the didactic and behavioral models, with its video-based lessons and its more behavioral-oriented exercises involving rapid feedback in basic mathematics exercises. The academy's computer science code talk-throughs combine the didactic practice of explanation and exposition on the audio track with a constructionist/constructivist experience of computer programming in real time. Students can switch between either mode in an instant. The MIT edX circuit design course embedded simulations within the video lectures so students could interactively explore abstract concepts in tangible ways.

No matter the base pedagogical strategy that motivated the development of each of these teaching machines, we have seen that they frequently share common elements: a structure that allows individualized pacing, a demand for mastery learning, a tendency to break up content into digestible bits, devices to provide rapid feedback, and an emphasis on adaptive learning and remedial instruction. Is there something fundamental to technology-assisted learning in these commonalities?

Individualized Pacing

It is little wonder that the concept of individualized pacing shows up as an attribute of almost all of the teaching machines explored in this book, with the exception of the synchronous radio and television broadcasts. It seems like a commonsense observation that people do not learn all subjects at the same rate and that a good instructor should try to meet students where they currently are academically. The ability to progress through instruction at their own pace can make students much more engaged in the learning process.

Individualized pacing allows learners to trade time for academic ability. Students who have already been exposed to the material, or have an affinity in a particular area, can move rapidly through the curriculum, while students who are less adept at the material can take the time needed without affecting overall class pacing. As the student from the 1963 Roanoke teaching machines study offered, "The eggheads don't get slowed up; the clods don't get showed up."[3]

The idea that people should learn the same things at the same time is primarily an artifact from the way classrooms have been organized by age since the mid-nineteenth century. Prior to that, students of all ages were grouped together in the proverbial "one-room schoolhouse," with as much as a 20-year spread between the oldest and youngest students. After the Civil War, schoolhouses were consolidated into the larger, age-graded schools we know today. It was thought that the lockstep environment might encourage scholarship because "the emulation of the pupils is excited, and effort is created. The higher grades draw up the lower ones." The teacher's task was to bring their pupils "up to grade," and academic success was required for a pupil to progress to the next grade. It was not until the 1940s when students were automatically progressed, often with little regard toward their academic achievement.[4]

The concept of synchronicity is the largest determiner of whether individualized pacing is possible for any given teaching machine. More asynchronous technologies like correspondence courses, online videos, and programmed instruction are typically more solitary learning experiences and generally do not have a large social component that synchronicity might engender.

The larger number of students in modern online learning experiences may provide an opportunity for learners to progress at their own pace through the curriculum and still develop a sense of community of support from fellow learners. There is no real reason to "show up for class" or finish an assignment at a given time if there is automated assessment or enough people taking the course to provide peer grading. The learner community may have an ever-changing population, but the large number of students should provide enough critical mass at any given time to support effective discussion and online help groups. Some MOOCs and e-learning efforts see a value in having a cohort working together over the potential benefits that individualized pacing might offer.

Mastery Learning

Mastery learning is a concept that appears in a number of teaching machines and encourages students to fully learn a given unit of curricular content before moving on to the next. It is particularly valuable when parts of the curriculum depend on knowledge gained from preceding lessons, such as in mathematics, science, and engineering. Some mathematics educators believe that the inability to fully master the concept of manipulating simple fractions in elementary school inhibits a student's chance of success in higher-level courses such as algebra.[5]

Henry Clinton Morrison is credited for popularizing the term when he headed up John Dewey's University of Chicago Laboratory Schools in the 1920s, saying, "When a student has fully acquired a piece of learning, he has mastered it. Half-learning, or learning rather well, or being on the way to learning are none of them mastery. Mastery implies completeness; the thing is done; the student has arrived. There is no question of how well the student has mastered it; he has either mastered it or he has not."[6] Some topics require a more thorough understanding than others. Although "C" may be a passing grade, I would definitely prefer that my airline pilot received an "A" on his landing skills test rather than even a "B."

Pressey and Skinner's teaching machines and the programmed instruction books made mastery learning a high priority, as do some serious games, intelligent tutoring systems, and the mathematics programs at Carnegie Learning and Khan Academy. Mastery learning works closely with the concept of individualized pacing, and it allows students to trade time for academic ability, while at the same time maintaining high academic standards for all students.

Content Granularity

Most of the teaching machines, with the exceptions of those built on constructionist, constructivist, or connectivist approaches, use a "divide-and-conquer" strategy to break up curricular content into more manageable and easily digestible chunks. The granularity, or fineness, of those chunks is usually dictated by the pedagogical framework the particular tool relies on.

While at the Laboratory Schools, Morrison also popularized the concept of unit mastery. He defined a *unit* as something that represented an element or aspect of a curricular subject "capable of being understood, rather than merely being remembered."[7] Textbooks have traditionally taken this approach, as have most of the teaching machines discussed here, including correspondence courses, broadcast and Internet-based instructional media, and MOOCs.

The mechanical teaching machines of Pressey and Skinner and the programmed instructional texts divided their curricular content into even finer portions than Morrison's definition of a unit. They used the technique of successive approximation, or shaping, to gradually lead a learner toward understanding the content by presenting it in a series of small, progressive steps. This technique can work quite well if a careful enough analysis of the material is done prior to transforming it into a well-designed progression. Unfortunately, the small steps in programmed instruction can be tedious for the learner, and often they inhibit larger contextual understanding if the progression is not effectively designed, as anecdotally evidenced in Holland and Skinner's *Analysis of Behavior* programmed textbook.

Rapid Feedback

The ability to provide almost instantaneous feedback is an advantage many modern teaching machines share. Rather than have students wait for their work to be corrected by hand, which may take days or even weeks, the learning process can be accelerated by the use of an automated assessment system. Indeed, Pressey believed his assessments could provide a secondary source of instruction. Rapid feedback moves assessment from the judgmental and often punitive *summative* mode to the more nurturing and supportive *formative* role in the learning process. There is ample research suggesting the importance of rapid feedback. According to cognitive scientist John Bransford, "In order for learners to gain insight into their learning and their understanding, frequent feedback is critical: students need to monitor their learning and actively evaluate their strategies and their current levels of understanding."[8]

The correspondence schools were hampered by the slow postal system of their days, which severely limited the speed in which they might respond, but to compensate, they streamlined the internal grading processes to return student grading and feedback as soon as they possibly could. Their more modern incarnations, the for-profit e-learning institutions, likewise place a high value on timely responses to student work and questions by limiting class sizes to provide it.

During that visit to his daughter's fourth-grade arithmetic class, B. F. Skinner was struck by how inefficient the feedback process was, saying, "Possibly through no fault of her own, the teacher was violating two fundamental principles: the students were not being told at once whether their work was right of wrong (a corrected paper seen twenty-four hours later could not act as a reinforcer), and they were all moving at the same pace regardless of preparation or ability." That week he constructed his first teaching machine to address those problems.[9]

MOOCs and the Khan Academy have actively tackled this issue with a variety of automated forms of grading, ranging from simple multiple-choice validation to more sophisticated "robo-grading" techniques, including automatic essay scoring and peer grading, such as UCLA's calibrated peer review. Current research is applying machine learning and data-mining techniques to the massive amount of student click-data these massive courses generate in order to discover other forms of automated assessment.

Adaptive Learning and Remedial Instruction

A good tutor typically has a dynamic, interactive, and reflexive relationship with his or her tutee. If the student does not understand something, the tutor might try to determine why, either by filling in gaps in understanding or explaining it in another way that might resonate better with them. To do this, the tutor must have a good understanding of what a student already knows and what she still needs to know, as well as a clear understanding of how the curricular content fits together. The tutor assesses the student's problem and instantly offers the right instruction that precisely addresses the deficit. After years of experience, effective tutors develop an informal *content map* of the content material in their heads. This is coupled with years of experience of seeing how other tutees have answered questions and struggled with learning the material, then developing insight into what may be the missing parts in their understandings.

There are unfortunately very few examples of teaching machines that have demonstrated this level of reflexivity. Most tools are capable of only a very rough understanding of what the student already knows, mainly through the blunt assessment tools of multiple-choice tests and answers to problem sets. These assessments can tell *if* the student understands the content but not *why*. To identify the why, a teaching machine must have a content map similar to what the tutor has, of how content parts connect with one another, have some notion of what the student already knows, and possess the ability to analyze what content parts are missing from an incorrect response. The system can then offer a new unit of remedial instruction to bridge the student's deficit.

Adaptive learning is similar, but it travels in the other direction. Rather than analyzing incorrect answers and remediating the instruction to make up for deficiencies, the system can deduce whether a student already understands any given content by comparing correct answers with the content map; if so, the system moves the student forward in the instructional sequence. This idea is in direct opposition to the behavioral-based teaching machines and programmed instruction books that plod along through the instruction regardless of whether or not the learner already knows it.

Adaptive and remedial instruction could theoretically be applied to any of the modern, computer-based teaching machines, but intelligent tutoring systems are one of the few systems to have successfully done so. They contain the internal constructs of a content map, a student model of what learners know, and the ability to guide them through an instruction sequence that respects their place within that content map.

Aside from a few canonical domains such computer languages, mathematics, and statistics, there has not been much development of ITS systems. The problem appears not primarily technological but practical. Creating detailed content maps of a content area is expensive and time consuming, as is developing assessments that can connect student responses to points on that content map for remediation or progression. The hope is that the large amounts of student data generated can serve as fodder for machine learning and data-mining to automatically generate these content maps and answer assessment tools.

Economies of Scale

Often, the purpose of technology is to increase the efficiency of tasks that people already perform. Riding a horse allowed people to travel faster and farther than they could have on foot. Attaching a plow to that horse enabled them to cultivate more land than they could have done by hand, and replacing that horse with a tractor further leveraged their time to be more efficient than not using that technology. From the industrial revolution to the Internet age, we have been applying the technology of our time to improve the economies of scale in our daily efforts.

If we are to take Benjamin Bloom at his word, that the best learning experience occurs as the result of one-to-one mastery tutoring,[10] and use that as the starting point, the typical American classroom with 25 students is a wildly efficient mechanism for leveraging an instructor's time. Unfortunately, that economic and temporal leverage also has a dilutive effect of the instructor's effectiveness in delivering instruction. As a result, most students taught in the traditional classroom learn significantly less than tutored students.

Almost all of the teaching machines explored here are exercises in using automation to scale education's efficiency. Some efforts, such as the intelligent tutoring systems, look to close the learning gap between the highly unleveraged one-to-one tutoring and traditional classroom instruction, whereas others merely seek to replicate the more modest traditional classroom instructional effectiveness through higher economies of scale.

The Chautauqua movement used printed curricular material delivered by the postal service to scale up the impact of their popular in-person event on Lake Chautauqua to a wider audience, and they organized local meetings to augment the feedback process. The correspondence schools streamlined that feedback process by employing an army of lower-paid people to rapidly grade and respond to student work without needing to hire a phalanx of more expensive instructors.

For-profit e-learning institutions would be wise to learn from the correspondence schools. Schools like the University of Phoenix still rely on very much the same process as the traditional classroom, with a single instructor providing instruction, grading, and feedback to a small number of students, albeit from a distance. Some economy of scale is offered by a standardized curriculum, but the instructor is not well leveraged in their current model.

The mechanical devices of Pressey and Skinner and Don Bitzer's PLATO system were answers to scaling instruction by making it more self-contained. Students sat at these teaching machines and received the instruction and assessment through the device itself, requiring no instructor attention, and they could scale based on the number of physical devices available. This of course was self-limiting in reality because the devices were expensive to purchase, but in principle, the mechanical/electronic teaching machines could scale infinitely.

The broadcast media of educational radio and television scale by their very nature, but only in one direction. It does not cost any more, or take any additional effort, to broadcast a lesson to 21,000 students than it does to 21. Broadcasting has the added potential to offer higher-quality instruction because the production costs can be spread over a larger number of students. The educational radio and television providers bypassed the issue of responding to student work by passing responsibility back to the teacher. MIT's OpenCourseWare uses a more modern delivery mechanism, the Internet, to deliver curricular content, but again, it offered no feedback mechanism to grade student work or answer student questions.

While one may argue that the pedagogies employed by MOOCs and the Khan Academy videos are primitive, these teaching machines do scale and have been effective at reaching millions of students. The Internet is undoubtedly the best curricular content delivery mechanism the world of teaching machines has ever known. With very little marginal cost, high-quality text, graphics, audio, video, and interactive content can be provided to learners anywhere, anytime. Online storage costs are so low, and there is such a wealth of external resources available with a mouse click that restricting curricular content because of its size is no longer an issue. There is virtually unlimited access to information.

As efficient a vehicle the Internet is for delivering curricular content, it does not address any of the issues involved in responding to student assignments and questions. If anything, the massive number of participants tends to exacerbate the problem. Providers have tried to address these issues with a combination of technology and social engineering, ranging from automated assessments and natural language-based essay scoring to various forms of peer-grading techniques and discussion forums. Business models may also evolve to include options for students to pay for personalized support as needed. The large amount of student-generated data has the potential through big-data and machine-learning approaches to offer automated responses to complex questions and provide a more nuanced assessment of higher-level thinking assignments.

Issues of scale affect not only the delivery of instruction but also its creation. If the curricular content that drives the teaching machine is too expensive or too time consuming to create, it makes any economies of scale that much more difficult. Teaching machines that employ consumer entertainment technologies, such as games and video, have demonstrated this challenge. It is hard to economically justify the millions of dollars regularly spent on high-end television and video game productions toward a much smaller target audience that cannot collectively pay to recover that investment. The cost and time required to produce high-quality programmed instruction with remedial instructional paths and develop sophisticated content models for adaptive learning tools for such instructional tutoring systems has resulted in a dearth of curricular content for these tools. Many of the systems can effectively deliver content that scales, but those systems are hampered from a lack of quality content to feed them.

As appealing as the ability to scale may be economically, the techniques that have proven most effective to scale tend to focus on lower-level thinking skills, such as elementary mathematics and the training of very specific skill sets. Trying to achieve economies of scale in higher-order thinking skills, such as problem-solving, has thus far proven immune to technological intervention. Classroom techniques that require an instructor's direct attention, such as Socratic teaching, or problem- and project-based learning, are very successful, but they cannot be expanded beyond a small number of students before becoming ineffective. Seymour Papert's connectivist approaches relied on a reflexive dialogue between the instructor and the student. However valuable that interpersonal interaction may be for the learning experience, it does not scale very well.

Diffusion of Innovations

One measure of the impact of any teaching machine is the extent to which it was adopted and used by its targeted constituency. The diffusion of innovations theory offers a time-tested framework to parse out some of the factors that may have contributed to an innovation's success or failure.

Rural sociologist Everett Rogers was instrumental in establishing this systematic study in the ways innovations are introduced to and adopted by potential users.

Rogers began his research over 50 years ago by studying the mechanisms by which American farmers successfully adopted the agricultural innovations developed at land-grant universities.* In a series of diffusion studies across multiple areas, Rogers found that innovations that have higher levels of these characteristics—high relative advantage, trialability, observability, and compatibility but low complexity—are likely to succeed over innovations that possess lower levels of those attributes.[11]

Relative advantage is the degree to which an innovation appears to be better than any other alternatives the potential adopter might have, measured in terms of economics, convenience, satisfaction, and social prestige. It is the abstraction of Ralph Waldo Emerson's "better mousetrap," and it has been identified as the most important predictor of an innovation's adoption rate. Innovations do not typically exist in a vacuum, and they therefore must compete with other innovations looking to serve the same purpose.

Correspondence courses, broadcast radio and television instruction, and e-learning efforts successfully competed with traditional classroom instruction on the basis of providing geographic and temporal mobility for their learners. Sidney Pressey and B. F. Skinner promised classroom teachers freedom from drudgery and faster learning times for their students. Seymour Papert suggested that students could learn higher-level thinking skills by using Logo in the classroom. And of course, it's hard to compete with free; MOOCs, MIT's OpenCourseWare, and the Khan Academy offer their content to learners at no charge and on demand.

Trialability is the degree in which the innovation can be experienced firsthand on a limited basis. For example, pills for weight control are certainly more triable than having one's stomach surgically tied and thus are tried with far more frequency, in spite of their limited effectiveness. The teaching machines of Pressey and Skinner required expensive specialized mechanical devices for each student to use, making them difficult to test.

---

*Land-grant universities are institutions of higher learning in all 50 states endowed by gifts of land by the U.S. government under the 1862 Morill Act, which formed the system of large, public universities.

The same was true with Don Bitzer's PLATO system, which required an expensive, custom-designed computer terminal connected to an equally expensive mainframe.

In contrast, educational radio and television could be tried by simply turning on an inexpensive device most people already owned. Likewise, the ease in downloading Khan Academy videos or instantly enrolling in a MOOC makes it simple for people to see, with very little effort, if it is a viable mechanism for learning for them. Triability of course contributes to low completion rates, when viewed as a percentage of original enrollees, but the absolute numbers are truly impressive.

Observability is the degree in which the innovation or its results can be seen by others likely to adopt it. If potential adopters are unaware of an innovation or do not see it being used by their peers, they are less likely to adopt it themselves. If a tree falls in a forest, does it make a sound? To make matters worse, some of the distance and e-learning innovations are done solitarily at home, giving little opportunity for others to observe their efforts.

Another factor of observability is how the popular press covers the innovation. The media paid far less attention to Sidney Pressey than they did to B.F. Skinner, so it was not unreasonable that Skinner had not even heard of Pressey's work on teaching machines some two decades earlier, and why Skinner's teaching machines received millions of dollars in funding while Pressey struggled to get his machine manufactured. This media presence has been amplified in more recent times, with the tremendous amount of coverage of MOOCs in mainstream media outlets such as the *New York Times* and CNN.

Compatibility is the degree to which an innovation is seen as consistent with existing values, previous experiences, and needs of the user. Innovations exist among other innovations and rest on the experiences potential adopters have had with other innovations and their personal values and beliefs. Some innovations may be seen as a part of a larger group of innovations, known as a *technology cluster*, and may be judged by potential adopters within the context of the group rather than individually.

The popularity of "smart board" projection systems in classrooms highlights this idea, as the electronic whiteboard fits squarely in the longstanding tradition of teachers writing on the chalkboard. Using a smart board, teachers remain in the dominant position at the front of the classroom, a position very compatible with their accustomed blackboard activity. Sometimes the concept of compatibility is interpreted in terms of a process or practice. The fact that most teaching machines espouse the idea of individualized pacing is fundamentally *incompatible* with the way the traditional age-progressed classroom is organized, and this makes it less likely to be adopted.

Complexity is the degree in which the innovation is seen as difficult to understand or use. Pressey's machines presented teachers with constant mechanical problems that hampered their classroom adoption. The correspondence courses relied on a more traditional delivery vehicle and made it easy, albeit slow, for students to interact with the school in terms of receiving curricular content and responding to assessments, and the Internet-based teaching machines have generally made it simple for students to participate in their courses.

The cognitive psychologist Donald Norman is perhaps the most visible advocate for improving the usability of things we interact with by making them easier to use and less complex. He has recently joined the world of MOOCs and is offering a course based on his seminal book on usability, *The Design of Everyday Things*. According to Norman, the usability of most tools can be dramatically improved if we pay attention to just five basic ideas:

1. *Provide consistent models* when a machine is first designed. There is an underlying methodology to the system's organization from the designer's point of view, but once the tool is completed, this methodology is just one of three possible understandings of that organization. Equally important are the way the designer's model is actually represented in the tool itself, as well as the learner's own understanding of how it is structured.

2. *Make features visible* and obvious to users to help them see which elements they can interact with. The designer chooses what features to make visible (*affordances*) and which ones are hidden or unavailable (*constraints*) at any given time. This interplay of affordances and constraints provides an opportunity to guide the learner to explore potentially useful features while ignoring superfluous ones. Too many options can be as stifling as too few, so a thoughtful and dynamic balance will improve a teaching machine's usability.

3. *Provide good mappings.* Prompt the user's actions to perform or to represent an activity that mirrors this activity's true nature. For example, a left-to-right slider control in a computer drawing program is more appropriate for setting the height of a box on the screen, than a slider oriented vertically.

4. *Offer good feedback* when the user performs an action; this is as important in the interface as it is in response to assessment. The teaching machine should acknowledge that action by providing immediate feedback to indicate what changes were made. This feedback can be visual or auditory to provide information about the internal state of the model. Like pedagogical feedback, this feedback is more effective when it is repeated, immediate, and consistent.

5. To err is human, so innovators must *design for humanity.* Learners will consistently do things the designer did not expect them to do. A good teaching machine will try to anticipate as many of these situations and deal with them proactively. Designers should try to make all appropriate actions reversible so if unforeseen actions occur (and they will), they can be undone with a minimum of effort on the user's behalf. It is also important to be aware of the limits of human beings in terms of short-term memory and perception and not expect them to do things that breach those limits.[12]

It is not just the teaching machine in its role as a delivery vehicle that can add complexity; the difficulty of creating the curricular content can also thwart the adoption of a teaching machine. Programmed instruction and intelligent tutoring systems were good vehicles for rapidly teaching some kinds of content, but the difficulty and expense in producing truly effective content reduced the number of high-quality lessons available. Likewise, the high cost and complexity of producing first-rate content has resulted in a dearth of exemplary educational video and computer games.

I was personally able to verify that Everett Rogers's five diffusion factors were as evident in educational technology as they have been in the multiple industries Rogers and his colleagues studied over the past half-century. In 2006, I conducted a study to examine the factors contributing to the successful diffusion of technological innovations in the K–12 classroom. I identified 37 potential diffusion factors and examined 43 educational technology innovations to see if they exhibited those characteristics.

I also rated how successful innovations were in the marketplace. Neural network and multiple regression analysis suggested that the same five factors that Rogers identified in his diffusion of innovations research were most likely to predict an educational innovation's chances of success in the market.[13]

The makers of teaching machines have shown varying levels of business acumen when marketing their devices to educators, and the newest breed of venture-capital-funded companies stands heads above the academics and engineers from previous innovations. But these companies' abilities to apply consumer marketing and popular media strategies to education may not be enough. The education marketplace is rigid and filled with failed ventures that, in spite of being good ideas, were never adopted. Rogers's diffusion work illustrates the basic factors that go beyond simple product marketing techniques and are required to facilitate true change in education. Innovators would be wise to understand that and position their products with these factors in mind.

The Politics of Teaching Machines

The role of the instructor changes when using a teaching machine. Instead of the traditional "sage on the stage" role they currently play, teachers must cede curricular content design and the learner's focus of attention to someone, or rather *something*, else. Like the teachers who balked at the centralized control of the curriculum during the American Samoan television experiment, instructors often resent the lack of input they have in defining the content their students will learn. With the student's focus of attention moved away from them and toward the machine, their new role of "guide on the side" can be foreign, alienating, and threatening. Like most people, teachers are resistant to change, especially when it is externally forced, proving that old French saying, "the only people who want change are wet babies."[14]

Skinner and Pressey made conciliatory statements about how teachers' lives would be relieved of classroom drudgery, and Khan assures them that flipping the classroom will free them to provide students individualized attention. Unfortunately, the introduction of teaching machines is often a top-down decision by school administrators, with little buy-in sought from the teachers, whose primary role in the classroom will be disrupted. While some teachers have embraced the concept of the flipped classroom and are using videos to provide some of the primary instruction, teachers on the whole have not been enthusiastic supporters of most teaching machines, both in K–12 and higher-educational institutions.

Educational technology advocates need to do a better job of selling their vision to the people who actually will be on the front lines of instruction rather than just the administration. The Roanoke teaching machines experiments were successful in part because Allen Calvin actively enlisted the support of the participating teachers. The Roanoke teachers helped develop the curricular content material and were heavily involved in planning the project.

Most universities use *time-in-class* as the primary measure of academic progress, not simple competency in the curricular content. Salman Khan did not need to attend his MIT classes in person in order to learn the same content as his fellow students, but he still needed to wait until the end of the semester to join them to take the final exam. The basic structure for earning college credits will need to change to a more competency-based system before technology-assisted teaching can compete on the same level as the status quo.

The predominance of the age-graded classroom is a natural limiter to teaching machines in K–12 education. The benefits provided by individual pacing are offset by the real logistics problem for classrooms that manage students by age as opposed to their academic progress. This is especially problematic because that progress might be uneven by discipline, with some students moving faster in one subject area than another.

The Economics of Teaching Machines

Education and money can often be strange bedfellows. There is an implied trust relationship between students and their instructor, not unlike the patient-doctor relationship. Both the patient and the student need to have faith that the doctor and instructor have his or her best interests at heart, and the introduction of money into the mix complicates this trust relationship unless it is openly acknowledged. Thomas Foster, president of the International Correspondence Schools, did not shy away from the fact that his company was in business to make money, commenting in 1906, "This is a commercial enterprise. It is necessarily so."[15] Foster's company provided an educational product that his students were willing to pay for, and he expected a profit in return.

The recent introduction of venture capital funding in education is more troubling than Foster's desire to make money on his efforts. Venture capital (VC) funding has the potential to rapidly grow companies, but I would argue that an educational enterprise should be handled differently than a typical Internet startup. The cavalier investment and abandonment cycle has been wildly successful in the technology sector, but education needs to base itself on a more stable and slower-growing foundation. The typical VC strategy of investing in ten companies in the hope that one of them will succeed necessarily introduces instability into the marketplace. Silicon Valley thrives on that volatility, but education may not.

This is not to say that all is well with the business of education as it currently stands. Institutions of higher education are asking students to pay more and more for an education whose cost is beginning to overshadow any expected returns on that student's investment. Colleges and universities stand at risk from MOOCs and other technology-driven efforts, particularly in the large classroom courses with hundreds of students. These classes have been the only way in which traditional classroom instruction can achieve any economies of scale, but they do so at the cost of effective instruction. If technology provides a way to reach these large numbers of students as effectively as, or even more effectively than, the lecture hall, it is only a matter of time until universities will have to respond.

The business model that universities rely on is overly dependent on these large courses to fund smaller classes, which is simply no longer financially defensible. These "cash cows" are currently propped up because they offer the coin of the realm of higher education: course credits toward a degree. But there are signs that this hegemony is yielding to more efficient and potentially more cost-effective forms of education, with some universities now offering college credit for MOOCs. It is hard to argue that their massive in-person lecture experience is any better than a technology-driven one, and as the technology and pedagogical practices improve, it is likely to be worse.

Making Sense of a Century of Teaching Machines

Mark Twain once said, "History doesn't repeat, but it rhymes,"[16] and the narrative of teaching machines in education is no exception. Each of the innovations explored in this book represents a distinct effort in using technology to provide education, bowing to the economic, political, and technological environments of its day. I hope I've been able to highlight some of the common themes that necessarily emerge when people try to solve the same basic problems, often largely unaware of other people's journeys down similar pathways. Each of the teaching machines offered ways to efficiently teach people by employing technology, to achieve economies of scale, better or faster instruction, better control the curriculum, and freedom from geographical and time constraints. That technology can be in the form of textbooks sent by mail or highly interactive computer applications delivered over the Internet.

One common thread here is the learner. With all due respect to those who claim a fundamental difference between the "digital natives" of our time and those who grew up in less technologically advanced eras, people in the age of MOOCs learn in pretty much the same way as they did in days of the Chautauquas. We need to respect that biological reality and pay attention to the more enduring characteristics that have evolved over millions of years, such as the limits of our short-term memory. Instruction needs to be more learner-centered than it is currently conducted in most technology-assisted education. The motto of the 1933 Chicago World's Fair was "Science Finds, Industry Applies, Man Conforms." But user-centered design advocate Don Norman has suggested a more humane mantra for applying technology to human problems and turning things around: "People Propose, Science Studies, Technology Conforms."[17]

It would be easy to be become disillusioned after looking at a century of mostly unsuccessful efforts in educational technology and viewing the effort as a Sisyphean effort, repeatedly doomed to failure. Some promising ideas may have arrived too early for the world they were born into. Whether that mismatch was economic, political, or technological, some of these pedagogical concepts and strategies may prove more fertile in today's environment.

At the risk of being yet another technologist proclaiming "this time it's different," this time it *is* different. The pace of change in technology is now rising exponentially, as opposed to the steady, linear pace of earlier times. The capabilities of computers are doubling every year or two, and the number of Internet users has risen 600 percent since 2000. Because of this multiplicative rate of change, the use of technology is likely to provide useful solutions to previously intractable problems. That intersection of the faster machines and the massive number of high-speed connections between them will enable new possibilities we cannot now predict.

In 1989, B. F. Skinner observed, "Computers are now much better teaching machines" than the technological devices of his era.[18] But it will take more than better machines to make an impact on education. Teaching machines can be only as effective as the pedagogical methods they employ, the way they are diffused to the public, and how they stay focused on the learner. By looking at the past, we can surely build more effective teaching machines for the future. The specifics may be different, but the overall ideas rhyme.

Notes

Chapter 1. Introduction

1. R. Heinich, M. Molenda, and J. D. Russell, *Instructional Media and the New Technologies of Instruction*, 3rd ed. (New York: Macmillan, 1989), cited in P. Saettler, *The Evolution of American Educational Technology* (Greenwich, CT: Information Age Publishing, 2004), p. 5.

2. A. Tuer, *History of the Horn-book* (New York: Charles Scribner & Sons, 1896).

3. C. Anderson et al., *Technology in American Education, 1650–1900* (Washington, DC: U.S. Department of Health, Education, and Welfare, Office of Education, 1896).

4. S. May, "American Educational Biography," *American Journal of Education* 6 (1866): 140–41.

5. P. Saettler, *The Evolution of American Educational Technology* (Greenwich, CT: Information Age Publishing, 2004).

6. *Catechism* (from the Greek for "sound down") is a method to impart a summary of the basic doctrines through an oral question-and-answer session.

7. J. Wakefield, "A Brief History of Textbooks: Where Have We Been All These Years?" Presented at Text and Academic Authors, St. Petersburg, Florida, June 1998.

8. A. W. Ward et al., *The Cambridge History of English and American Literature: An Encyclopedia in 18 Volumes* (New York: Putnam, 1907–21), vol. 18, p. 25.

9. Wakefield, "Brief History of Textbooks."

10. H. Black, *The American Schoolbook* (New York: William Morrow, 1967), pp. 127–41.

11. Ibid.

12. Ibid., p. 132.

13. J. Kett, *The Pursuit of Knowledge Under Difficulties: From Self-Improvement to Adult Education in America, 1750–1990* (Stanford, CA: Stanford University Press, 1994), p. 80.

14. K. Silber, *Pestalozzi: The Man and His Work*, 2nd ed. (London: Routledge & Kegan Paul, 1965), p. 136.

15. G. Nash, "Creating History Standards in United States and World History," *OAH Magazine of History* 9, no. 3 (1995): 3.

16. G. Nash and C. Crabtree, *History on Trial: Culture Wars and the Teaching of the Past* (New York: Knopf, 1997).

17. 141 Cong. Rec. S.Res. 66 (1995): S1290.

18. E. Rogers, *Diffusion of Innovations*, 4th ed. (New York: Free Press, 1995), pp. 261–68.

19. Annie E. Casey Foundation, *KIDS COUNT Data Center*, http://datacenter.kidscount.org.

20. National Center for Education Statistics. *Digest of Education Statistics, 2011* (Washington, DC: U.S. Department of Education, 2011), table 349.

21. B. Rampey, G. Dion, and P. Donahue, *NAEP 2008 Trends in Academic Progress* (Washington, DC: National Center for Education Statistics, Institute of Education Sciences, U.S. Department of Education, 2009).

22. W. Bowen, "The 'Cost Disease' in Higher Education: Is Technology the Answer?" Presented at the Tanner Lectures, Stanford University, Stanford, California, October 2012.

23. R. Frank, "The Prestige Chase Is Raising College Costs," *New York Times*, Mar. 10, 2012.

24. M. Kinzie et al. "Designing Effective Curricula and Teacher Professional Development for Early Childhood Mathematics and Science," in *Effective Early Childhood Professional Development: Improving Teacher Practice and Child Outcomes*, ed. C. Howes, B. Hamre, and R. Pianta, National Center for Research in Early Childhood Education (Baltimore, MD: Paul H. Brookes, 2012).

25. T. Oppenheimer, *The Flickering Mind: The False Promise of Technology in the Classroom and How Learning Can Be Saved* (New York: Random House, 2003).

26. The figure of 60 million students comes from the *Digest of Education Statistics* (2010), http://nces.ed.gov/programs/digest/d10/tables/dt10_002.asp.

27. D. Norman, *The Design of Everyday Things* (New York: Basic Books, 1988), p. 9.

28. A. Tuer, *History of the Horn-book* (New York: Charles Scribner's Sons, 1896).

29. C. Shirk, "Napster, Udacity, and the Academy" (Nov. 12, 2012), retrieved from http://shirky.com/weblog.

30. D. Koller, personal communication, Feb. 20, 2013.

31. L. Cuban, *Teachers and Machines: The Classroom Use of Technology since 1920* (New York: Teachers College Press, 1986), p. 2.

32. From data provided by Coursera, personal communication, June 1, 2013.

33. G. Moore, "Cramming More Components onto Integrated Circuits," *Electronics* 38, no. 8 (1965): 52–59.

34. K. Zickuhr and A. Smith, "Digital Differences" (2012), Pew Internet and American Life Project, retrieved from www.pewinternet.org/~/media//Files/Reports/2012/PIP_Digital_differences_041312.pdf.

Chapter 2. Sage on the Stage

1. M. McLuhan, *Understanding Media: The Extensions of Man* (New York: McGraw-Hill, 1964), p. 289.

2. A. King, "From Sage on the Stage to Guide on the Side," *College Teaching* 41, no. 1(1993): 30–35.

3. M. Moore, *From Chautauqua to the Virtual University: A Century of Distance Education in the United States*, Information Series no. 393 (Columbus: Center on Education and Training for Employment, College of Education, Ohio State University, 2003), retrieved from http://www.cete.org/acve/docs/distance.pdf.

4. A. Bestor, *Chautauqua Publications: An Historical and Biographical Guide* (Chautauqua, NY: Chautauqua Press, 1934), p. 1.

5. J. Kett, *The Pursuit of Knowledge under Difficulties: From Self-Improvement to Adult Education in America, 1750–1990* (Stanford, CA: Stanford University Press, 1994), p. 156.

6. Ibid., p. 158.

7. L. Vincent, *John Heyl Vincent: A Biographical Sketch* (New York: Macmillan, 1925), p. 117.

8. Ibid., p. 118.

9. Ibid., p. 117.

10. J. Vincent, *The Chautauqua Movement* (Freeport, NY: Books for Libraries Press, 1971).

11. H. Oyen, "The Founder of 'Chautauquas'" in *The World's Work: A History of Our Time XXIV May–October*, ed. W. Page and A. Page (New York: Doubleday, 1912), p. 101.

12. A. Hyde, *The Story of Methodism* (Greenfield, MA: Wiley, 1897), pp. 444–58.

13. Kett, *Pursuit of Knowledge*, p. 157.

14. Hyde, *Story of Methodism*, pp. 20–49.

15. Ibid., pp. 451–55.

16. Vincent, *John Heyl Vincent*, pp. 140–42.

17. Bestor, *Chautauqua Publications*, p. 5.

18. Oyen, "Founder of 'Chautauquas.'"

19. Kett, *Pursuit of Knowledge*, p. 161.

20. J. Clark, "The Correspondence School—Its Relation to Technical Education and Some of Its Results," *Science* 24, no. 611 (Sept. 14, 1906): 327–34.

21. According to the Open Education database at http://oedb.org/rankings/graduation-rate.

22. S. Kolowich, "Coursera Takes a Nuanced View of MOOC Dropout Rates," *Chronicle of Higher Education*, June 5, 2013, retrieved from http://chronicle.com/blogs/wiredcampus/coursera-takes-a-nuanced-view-of-mooc-dropout-rates.

23. Bestor, *Chautauqua Publications*, p. 12.

24. J. Noffsinger, *Correspondence Schools, Lyceums, Chautauquas* (New York: MacMillan, 1926), p. 12.

25. International Correspondence Schools (ICS), "Thomas J. Foster's Quest for Mining Safety Becomes Largest Home Study School in the World," press release (1990), p. 1.

26. J. Watkinson, "Educating the Million: Education, Institutions, and the Working Class, 1787–1920" (PhD diss., University of Virginia, 1995), p. 174.

27. ICS, "Thomas J. Foster's Quest," p. 2.

28. T. Foster, "Instruction by Correspondence," *American Machinist* 29 (1906): 583–87.

29. ICS, "Thomas J. Foster's Quest," p. 2.

30. Foster, "Instruction by Correspondence," p. 586.

31. Ibid.

32. Clark, "Correspondence School," p. 329.

33. Watkinson, "Educating the Million," p. 177.

34. Foster, "Instruction by Correspondence," p. 583.

35. Ibid., p. 585.

36. Kett, *Pursuit of Knowledge*, p. 254.

37. Watkinson, "Educating the Million," p. 177.

38. Noffsinger, *Correspondence Schools*, p. 67.

39. Foster, "Instruction by Correspondence," p. 587.

40. A. Eisenberg, "Keeping an Eye on Online Test-Takers," *New York Times*, Mar. 3, 2013, retrieved from www.nytimes.com/2013/03/03/technology/new-technologies-aim-to-foil-online-course-cheating.html.

41. Foster, "Instruction by Correspondence," p. 584.

42. Ibid., p. 587.

43. Kett, *Pursuit of Knowledge*, pp. 236–37.

44. Watkinson, "Educating the Million," pp. 187–88.

45. Ibid.

46. Clark, "Correspondence School," p. 332; Noffsinger, *Correspondence Schools*, p. 66.

47. Clark, "Correspondence School," p. 332.

48. Kett, *Pursuit of Knowledge*, p. 586.

49. C. Tomlinson, "Mapping a Route toward Differentiated Instruction," *Educational Leadership* 57, no. 1 (1999): 12–16.

50. P. Saettler, *The Evolution of American Educational Technology* (Greenwich, CT: Information Age Publishing, 2004), p. 98.

51. Ibid., pp. 98–99.

52. Ibid.

53. G. Alexander, *Academic Films for the Classroom: A History* (Jefferson, NC: McFarland, 2010), p. 15.

54. "National Archives and Records Service Film-Vault Fire at Suitland, MD: Hearings before a Subcommittee of the Committee on Government Operations, House of Representatives, Ninety-Sixth Congress, First Session, June 19 and 21, 1979," retrieved from http://archive.org/stream/nationalarchivesoounitrich/nationalarchivesoounitrich_djvu.txt

55. Alexander, *Academic Films*, pp. 16–17.

56. Ibid., p. 22.

57. W. Bianchi, "Education by Radio: Schools of the Air," *TechTrends: Linking Research and Practice to Improve Learning* 52, no. 2 (2008): 36–44.

58. Saettler, *Evolution of American Educational Technology*, pp. 197–99.

59. Ibid.

60. B. Darrow, "Tub" (U.S. Patent 1,590,738, issued June 29, 1926); W. Bianchi, *Schools of the Air: A History of Instructional Programs on Radio in the United States* (Jefferson, NC: McFarland, 2008), p. 21,

61. B. Darrow, "Geographical Globe" (U.S. Patent no. 2,466,581, issued Apr. 5, 1949).

62. Bianchi, "Education by Radio," p. 39.

63. W. Schramm, *Big Media, Little Media: Tools and Technologies for Instruction* (Beverly Hills, CA: Sage, 1977), pp. 33–58.

64. J. Murphy and R. Gross, *Learning by Television* (New York: Fund for the Advancement of Education, 1966), pp. 10–12.

65. Ford Foundation, *Teaching by Television: A Report from the Ford Foundation and the Fund for the Advancement of Education* (New York: Ford Foundation, 1961), p. 29.

66. Ibid., p. 15.

67. J. Bergmannand and A. Sams, *Flip Your Classroom: Reach Every Student in Every Class Every Day* (Eugene, OR: International Society for Technology in Education, 2012).

68. W. Schramm, *Bold Experiment: The Story of Educational Television in American Samoa* (Stanford, CA: Stanford University Press, 1981), pp. 6–11.

69. Ibid., p. 80.

70. The German navy invaded a Samoan village in 1889 and destroyed some American property, promoting the United States to send some ships in retaliation. A typhoon

destroyed both the German and U.S. ships before any fighting started, and an armistice was called. See Robert Louis Stevenson, *A Footnote to History: Eight Years of Trouble in Samoa* (New York: Charles Scribner's Sons, 1900).

71. National Governors Association, "American Samoa Governor Hyrum Rex Lee," retrieved from www.nga.org/cms/home/governors/past-governors-bios/page_american_samoa/col2-content/main-content-list/title_lee_hyrum.html.

72. H. Lee, "Planning Communications Facilities for Public Education," *Annals of the New York Academy of Sciences*, 142 (March 1967): 531–38.

73. Schramm, *Bold Experiment*, p. 26.

74. Lee, "Planning Communications Facilities," pp. 531.

75. Schramm, *Bold Experiment*, pp. 16–25.

76. Lee, "Planning Communications Facilities," pp. 531–32.

77. Schramm, *Bold experiment*, pp. 35–55.

78. Ibid., pp. 77, 74.

79. Ibid., p. 88.

80. Ibid., p. 80.

81. P. Mishra and M. Koehler, "Technological Pedagogical Content Knowledge: A Framework for Teacher Knowledge," *Teachers College Record*, 108, no. 6 (2006): 1017–54.

82. C. Rose (producer), segment on *60 Minutes*, CBS, May 12, 2013.

83. K. Bales, "Ivy League Courses for the Price of a Video," *New York Times*, Feb. 16, 1994, retrieved from www.nytimes.com/1994/02/16/news/16iht-videduc.html.

84. Great Courses, "About Us" (2013), retrieved from www.thegreatcourses.com/tgc/about%20us/home.aspx.

85. S. Wooley, "Raw and Random," *Forbes*, Mar. 3, 2006, retrieved from www.forbes.com/global/2006/0313/027.html.

86. See http://ed.ted.com.

87. C. Goldberg, "Auditing Classes at M.I.T. on the Web and Free," *New York Times*, Apr. 4, 2001.

88. L. Johnson, "Q&A with Professor Hal Abelson of MIT" (2009), retrieved from http://research.google.com/university/relations/visiting-faculty/professor-hal-abelson.html.

89. MIT Computer Science and Artificial Intelligence Laboratory, "People" (2012), retrieved from http://www.csail.mit.edu/user/1535.

90. H. Abelson, "The Creation of OpenCourseWare at MIT," *Journal of Science Education and Technology* 17, no. 2 (2008): 164–65.

91. C. Vest, "MIT OpenCourseWare: Past Present and Future" (presented at Open Courseware, Open Futures: Where Is Michigan?, University of Michigan, Ann Arbor, Oct. 5, 2007), video file retrieved from http://deepblue.lib.umich.edu/handle/2027.42/58058.

92. Goldberg, "Auditing Classes."

93. Vest, "MIT OpenCourseWare."

94. "Mellon, Hewlett Foundations Grant $11M to Launch Free MIT Course Materials on Web" (press release, June 18, 2001), retrieved from http://web.mit.edu/newsoffice/2001/ocwfund.html.

95. Ibid.

96. MIT OpenCourseWare, "Site Statistics" (June 21, 2013), retrieved from http://ocw.mit.edu/about/site-statistics.

97. Retrieved from www.parchment.com/c/college/college-762-Massachusetts-Institute-of-Technology.html.

98. N. Negroponte, *Being Digital* (New York: Knopf, 1995), p. 18.

99. S. Lonn and S. Teasley, "Podcasting in Higher Education: What Are the Implications for Teaching and Learning?" *Internet and Higher Education* 12, no. 2 (2009): 88–92.

Chapter 3. Step by Step

1. S. Pressey, "Sidney Leavitt Pressey," in *A History of Psychology in Autobiography, vol. 5*, ed. E. Boringa and G. Lindzey (East Norwalk CT: Appleton-Century-Crofts, 1967), pp. 313–16.

2. S. Pressey, "Sidney Leavitt Pressey: An Autobiography," in *Leaders in American Education Part 1*, ed. Robert J. Havighurst (Chicago: University of Chicago Press, 1971), p. 233.

3. S. Petrina, "Sidney Pressey and the Automation of Education, 1924–1934," *Technology and Culture* 45, no. 2 (2004): 310.

4. Pressey, "Autobiography," pp. 319–20.

5. W. Harms and I. DePencier, *Experiencing Education: 100 Years of Learning at the University of Chicago Laboratory Schools* (Chicago: University of Chicago Laboratory Schools, 1996).

6. L. Vincent, *John Heyl Vincent: A Biographical Sketch* (New York: Macmillan, 1925), p. 130.

7. W. Urban and J. Wagoner, *American Education: A History* (New York: McGraw-Hill, 2000).

8. L. Benjamin, "A History of Teaching Machines," *American Psychologist* 43, no. 9 (1988): 707.

9. H. Skinner, "Improvement in Apparatus for Teaching Spelling" (U.S. Patent no. 52,758, issued Feb. 20, 1866); "Halcyon Skinner Killed," *New York Times*, Nov. 29, 1900, retrieved from http://query.nytimes.com/gst/abstract.html?res=F00B14F8385A16738DDDA00A94D9415B808CF1D3#.

10. Benjamin, "History of Teaching Machines," p. 704.

11. Petrina, "Sidney Pressey and the Automation of Education," pp. 328–29.

12. E. Boring, "CP Speaks," *Contemporary Psychology* 3, no. 6 (1958): 152–53.

13. J. Anderson, "Proceedings of the Thirty-Third Annual Meeting of the American Psychological Association," *Psychological Bulletin* 22, no. 2 (1925): 111.

14. According to www.apa.org/convention/about/faqs.

15. Anderson, "Procedings," p. 68.

16. S. Pressey, "Machine for Intelligence Tests" (U.S. Patent no. 1,670,480, filed Jan. 30, 1926, issued May 22, 1928).

17. S. Pressey, "A Simple Apparatus which Gives Tests and Scores—and Teaches," *School and Society* 23, no. 586 (1926): 374.

18. Ibid.

19. C. Foltz, *The World of Teaching Machines: Programed Learning and Self-Instructional Devices* (Washington, DC: Teaching Research and Technology Division, Electronic Teaching Laboratories, 1961), p. 35.

20. Petrina, "Sidney Pressey and the Automation of Education," p. 310.

21. L. Cremin, *The Transformation of the American School* (New York: Knopf, 1961), pp. 110–13.

22. Ludy Benjamin, personal communication, Aug. 25, 2013.

23. E. Thorndike, *Education: A First Book* (New York: Macmillan, 1912), p. 65.

24. S. Pressey, "A Machine for Automatic Teaching of Drill Material," *School and Society* 25, no. 645 (1927): 551–52.

25. Petrina, "Sidney Pressey and the Automation of Education," p. 313.

26. Ibid.

27. Ibid., p. 317.

28. Ibid.

29. Ibid., p. 318.

30. Pressey, "Autobiography," p. 323.

31. S. Pressey, "A Third and Fourth Contribution toward the Coming 'Industrial Revolution' in Education," *School and Society* 36, no. 934 (1932): 672.

32. B. Skinner, "Teaching Machines," *Science* 128, no. 3330 (1958): 969.

33. A. Coladarci, "Sidney Pressey to Receive First E. L. Thorndike Award," *Educational Psychologist* 1, no. 1 (1963).

34. B. Skinner, *The Particulars of My Life* (New York: McGraw-Hill, 1977), pp. 67–68.

35. See advertising to develop public esteem for Practipedists in *Printers' Ink*, Apr. 1, 1920, p. 111, retrieved from http://books.google.com/books?id=ab9DN5JUMW4C&pg=111.

36. Skinner, *Particulars*, p. 166.

37. Ibid., p. 36.

38. Ibid., pp. 183–84.

39. Ibid., pp. 227–28.

40. Ibid., p. 247.

41. Ibid., p. 249.

42. Ibid., p. 301.

43. B. Skinner, *The Shaping of a Behaviorist* (New York: Knopf, 1979), pp. 24–31.

44. B. Skinner, "A Case History in Scientific Method," *American Psychologist* 11, no. 5 (1956): 221–33.

45. Skinner, *Shaping of a Behaviorist*, p. 80.

46. Ibid., p. 87.

47. B. Ludy and E. Nielsen-Gammon, "B. F. Skinner and Psychotechnology: The Case of the Heir Conditioner," *Review of General Psychology* 3, no. 3 (1999): 157.

48. B. F. Skinner, "Baby in a Box," *Ladies Home Journal*, Oct. 1945, p. 30.

49. J. Vargas, "A Brief Biography of B. F. Skinner" (2005), retrieved from http://bfskinner.org/about-b-f-skinner-2/.

50. Benjamin, "B. F. Skinner and Psychotechnology," pp. 160–61.

51. Skinner, *Particulars*, p. 292.

52. Marilyn Gilbert, personal communication, July 8, 2013.

53. B. Skinner, "Pigeons in a Pelican," *American Psychologist* 15, no. 1 (1960): 28.

54. C. Ferster, *Behavior Principles* (Englewood, NJ: Prentice-Hall, 1982), p. 9.

55. See "Project Pigeon (Orcon)" (silent video), retrieved from http://bfskinner.org/project-pigeon/.

56. Skinner, "Pigeons in a Pelican," p. 31, 37.

57. Skinner, "Shaping of a Behaviorist," p. 80.

58. B. Skinner, *A Matter of Consequences* (New York: Knopf, 1983), p. 64.

59. Ibid., pp. 69–70.

60. B. Skinner, "The Science of Learning and the Art of Teaching," *Harvard Educational Review* 2 (Nov. 2, 1954): 110.

61. Skinner, *Matter of Consequences*, pp. 69–70.

62. Benjamin, *History of Teaching Machines*, p. 708.

63. E. Boring, "CP speaks," *Contemporary Psychology* 2, no. 23 (1957): 312–13.

64. Boring, "CP Speaks" (1958), pp. 152–53.

65. P. Young, *Teaching, Learning, and the Mind* (Boston: Houghton-Mifflin, 1973), pp. 94–95.

66. B. Skinner, "Reflections on a Decade of Teaching Machines," in *Teaching Machines and Programmed Learning*, ed. R. Glaser (Washington, DC: National Education Association, 1965), p. 7.

67. Plato, *Meno* (380 BCE), trans. Benjamin Jowett, retrieved from http://classics.mit.edu/Plato/meno.html.

68. I. Cohen, "Programmed Learning and the Socratic Dialogue," *American Psychologist* 17, no. 11 (1962): 772–75.

69. J. Holland, "Teaching Machines: An Application of Principles from the Laboratory," *Journal of Experimental Analysis Behavior* 3, no. 4 (1960): 279.

70. E. Guba, "Teaching Machines Are Here to Stay," *Theory into Practice* 1, no. 1 (1962): 6.

71. E. Bozhovich, "Zone of Proximal Development: The Diagnostic Capabilities and Limitations of Indirect Collaboration," *Journal of Russian and East European Psychology* 47, no. 6 (2009): 48–69, 49.

72. J. Guthrie, "Morrison, Henry C. (1871–1945)," in *Encyclopedia of Education, vol. 2*, 2d ed. (New York: Macmillan Reference, 2003), pp. 1689–90.

73. H. Beck, "The Contributions of Henry Clinton Morrison: An Educational Administrator at Work" (PhD diss., University of Chicago, 1962), p. 124.

74. Skinner, "Matter of Consequences," pp. 69–70.

75. G. Williamson, *Memoirs of My Years with IBM: 1951–1986* (Bloomington, IN: Xlibris, 2008), p. 160.

76. Skinner, "Matter of Consequences," pp. 97–98.

77. B. Skinner, "Programmed Instruction Revisited," *Phi Delta Kappan*, Oct. 1986, p. 104.

78. Skinner, "Matter of Consequences," pp. 158–89.

79. Thorndike, *Education*, p. 65.

80. J. Holland and B. Skinner, *The Analysis of Behavior: A Program for Self-Instruction* (New York: McGraw-Hill, 1961).

81. J. Bell, "Will Robots Teach Your Children?" *Popular Mechanics*, Oct. 1961, pp. 152–57; G. Boehm, "Can People Be Taught Like Pigeons?" *Fortune*, Oct. 1960, p. 260.

82. Skinner, "Teaching Machines," p. 971.

83. S. Pressey and J. Kinzer, "Auto-elucidation without Programing!" *Psychology in the Schools* 1, no. 4 (1964): 360–61.

84. B. Fine, *Teaching Machines* (New York: Sterling, 1962), p. 57.

85. C. S. Morrill, "Teaching Machines: A Review," *Psychological Bulletin* 58, no. 5 (1961): 369.

86. Boehm, "Can People Be Taught Like Pigeons?" p. 260.

87. Gilbert, personal communication.

88. R. Dudney, "When Sputnik Shocked the World," *Air Force Magazine* 90, no. 10 (Oct. 2007): 42–47.

89. H. Rickover, *Education and Freedom* (New York: Dutton, 1959), p. 6.

90. M. Hiatt and C. Stockton, "The Impact of the Flexner Report on the Fate of Medical Schools in North America after 1909," *Journal of the American Medical Association* 291, no. 17 (2003): 2139–40.

91. E. Johanningmeier, "A Nation at Risk and Sputnik," *American Educational History Journal* 37, no. 2 (2010): 347–65.

92. P. Saettler, *The Evolution of American Educational Technology* (Greenwich, CT: Information Age Publishing, 2004), pp. 412–15.

93. J. Finn and D. Perrin, *Teaching Machines and Programmed Learning* (Washington, DC: U.S. Office of Education, 1962), pp. 35–47.

94. R. Escobar and K. Lattal, "Observing Ben Wyckoff: From Basic Research to Programmed Instruction and Social Issues," *Behavior Analyst* 34, no. 2 (2011): 149–51.

95. Fine, *Teaching Machines*, p. 147

96. "The Teaching Machines," *Time Magazine* 79, no. 19 (1960): 89.

97. Escobar and Lattal, "Observing Ben Wyckoff," p. 157.

98. D. Tyack, *One Best System: A History of American Urban Education* (Cambridge, MA: Harvard University Press, 1974), pp. 269–75.

99. L. Hanson and P. Komoski, "School Use of Programmed Instruction," in *Teaching Machines and Programed Learning II: Data and Directions*, ed. R. Glaser (Washington, DC: National Education Association, 1965), p. 654.

100. "$68,000 Carnegie Grant Made for Hollins Test of Teaching Machines," *Hollins Herald* (Roanoke, VA), Mar. 1960.

101. E. Rushton, *Programmed Learning: The Roanoke Experiment* (Chicago: Encyclopaedia Britannica Press, 1965), p. 6.

102. Hanson and Komoski, "School Use of Programmed Instruction," pp. 654–55.

103. Rushton, *Programmed Learning*, pp. 17–18.

104. Ibid., pp. 23–26.

105. Ibid., p. 37.

106. "Hollins–E.B.F. Plan Math Series," *Hollins Herald*, May 1960.

107. "Trustees Turn Down EBF Proposal for Institute," *Hollins College Bulletin* 11, no. 5 (Mar. 1961): 1.

108. "EBF Center Now Located in California," *Hollins Columns*, Sept. 21, 1961.

109. Jan Everote (EBF president Warren Everote's daughter), personal communication, Apr. 3, 2013.

110. J. Wilson, *Banneker: A Case Study in Educational Change* (Homewood, IL: ETC Publications, 1973), pp. 13–29.

111. J. Ballentine and J. Spade, *Schools and Society: A Sociological Approach to Education* (Thousand Oaks, CA: Sage Publications, 2008), pp. 497–98.

112. J. Dinsmoor, "Studies in the History of Psychology CVI: An Appreciation of Fred S. Keller, 1899–1996," *Psychological Reports* 79, no. 3 (1996): 896.

113. F. Keller, "Good-Bye, Teacher . . . ," *Journal of Applied Behavior Analysis* 1, no. 1 (1968): 79–89.

114. K. Komoski, "Programmed Learning," *Time* 77, no. 13 (1961): 38.

115. N. Crowder, "On the Differences between Linear and Intrinsic Programming," *Phi Delta Kappan* 44, no. 6 (1963): 225–54.

116. J. Searle, "Minds, Brains, and Programs," *Behavioral and Brain Sciences* 3, no. 3 (1980): 417–58.

117. Foltz, *World of Teaching Machines*, p. 26.

118. B. Skinner, "Teaching Machines," *Science* 243, no. 4898 (Mar. 24, 1989): 1535.

Chapter 4. Byte by Byte

1. D. Hofstadter, *Gödel, Escher, Bach: The Eternal Braid* (New York: Vintage, 1989), p. 25.

2. Donald L. Bitzer, personal communication, Aug. 15, 2013.

3. "PLATO@50: A Culture of Innovation" (video, 80 min., recorded June 2, 2010), retrieved from www.platohistory.org/blog/2010/06/plato50-culture-of-innovation-panel -video.html.

4. Ibid.

5. Ibid.

6. E. Reilly, *Milestones in Computer Science and Information Technology* (Westport, CT: Greenwood Press, 2003), p. 132.

7. D. Albert and D. Bitzer, "Advances in Computer-Based Education," *Science* 167 (Mar. 20, 1970): 1586.

8. Ibid., p. 1584.

9. D. Bitzer, P. Braunfeld, and W. Lichtenberger, "PLATO: An Automatic Teaching Device," *IRE Transactions on Education* 4, no. 4 (1961): pp. 158–60.

10. Albert and Bitzer, "Advances in Computer-Based Education," p. 1587.

11. B. Sherwood, *The TUTOR Language* (Urbana IL: Plato Publications, 1974), p. 4.

12. D. Bitzer, B. Sherwood, and P. Tenczar, *Computer-Based Science Education* (Urbana, IL: CERL, 1973), p. 16.

13. Sherwood, *TUTOR Language*, p. 18–20.

14. "New National Inventors Hall of Fame Inductees Received Vital NSF Support" (news release, U.S. National Science Foundation, May 1, 2013), retrieved from www.nsf .gov/news/news_summ.jsp?cntn_id=127771. The NSF also funded a high-profile CAI project with a $4.5 million grant to the Mitre Corporation to develop the TICCIT system, which used a more centralized method of authoring courses for community college students; see A. Hammond, "Computer-assisted Instruction: Two Major Demonstrations," *Science* 176 (June 9, 1972): 1110.

15. Albert and Bitzer, "Advances in Computer-Based Education," p. 1586.

16. "PLATO@50."

17. R. Murphy and L. Appel, "Evaluation of the PLATO IV Computer-Based Education System in the Community College," *ACM SIGGCUE Bulletin* 12, no. 1 (1978): 20.

18. R. Clark, "Media Will Never Influence Learning," *Educational Technology Research and Development* 42, no. 2 (1994): 21.

19. For Edmentum, see www.edmentum.com/products-services/plato-courseware; for Pearson Digital Learning, see www.k12pearson.com/teach_learn_cycle/DL/dgtllrng .html.

20. E. Johanningmeier, "A Nation at Risk and Sputnik," *American Educational History Journal* 37, no. 2 (2010): 347–65.

21. R. Taylor, introduction to *The Computer in the School: Tutor, Tool, Tutee* (New York: Teachers College Press, 1980), pp. 7–10.

22. S. Papert, *Mindstorms: Children, Computers, and Powerful Ideas* (New York: Basic Books, 1993), pp. xviii–xxi.

23. S. Papert, *The Children's Machine: Rethinking School in the Age of the Computer* (New York: Basic Books, 1993), pp. 32–34.

24. Papert, *Mindstorms*, p. 23.

25. E. Ackermann, "Piaget's Constructivism, Papert's Constructionism: What's the Difference?" *Constructivism: Uses and Perspectives in Education, Conference Proceedings* (Geneva Research Center in Education, 2001), pp. 85–94.

26. Papert, *Mindstorms*, pp. 7–27.

27. Ackermann, "Piaget's Constructivism," p. 90.

28. Papert, *Mindstorms*, p. 125.

29. P. Saettler, *The Evolution of American Educational Technology* (Greenwich, CT: Information Age Publishing, 2004), p. 335.

30. Papert, *Mindstorms*, pp. 75–102.

31. Ibid., p. 103.

32. S. Papert, "Computer Criticism vs. Technocentric Thinking," *Educational Researcher* 16, no. 1 (1987): 23.

33. S. Papert, "You Can't Think about Thinking without Thinking about Something," *Contemporary Issues in Technology and Teacher Education* 5, nos. 3–4 (2005): 366–67.

34. S. Papert, "Tomorrow's Classrooms?" *New York Times Educational Supplement*, Mar. 5, 1982, p. 32.

35. N. Caftori, "Educational Software: Are We Approaching It the Right Way?" in *Proceedings of Society for Information Technology and Teacher Education International Conference*, ed. B. Robin et al. (Charlottesville, VA: Association for the Advancement of Computing in Education, 1996), p. 902.

36. S. Greenstein and M. Devereux, *The Crisis at Encyclopaedia Britannica* (Kellogg School of Management, Northwestern University, 2009), p. 7, retrieved from www.kellogg .northwestern.edu/faculty/greenstein/images/htm/Research/Cases/Encyclopaedia Britannica.pdf.

37. Ibid., pp. 10–14.

38. C. Shuler, "Where in the World Is Carmen Sandiego?" *The Edutainment Era: Debunking Myths and Sharing Lessons Learned* (New York: Joan Ganz Cooney Center at Sesame Workshop, 2012).

39. E. Klopfer and S. Osterweil, "The Boom and Bust and Boom of Educational Games," in *Transactions on Edutainment IX*, ed. Z. Pan et al. (New York: Springer, 2013), p. 291.

40. B. Sawyer, "Ben Sawyer on Games beyond Entertainment: Observations, Ideas, and Frameworks for Future Serious Games" (MIT Media lab lecture, 2009), retrieved from www.media.mit.edu/events/movies/video.php?id=sawyer-2009-03-19.

41. Ben Sawyer, personal communication, Aug. 15, 2013.

42. J. Gee, *What Video Games Have to Teach Us about Learning and Literacy* (New York: Palgrave Macmillan, 2007).

43. M. Prensky, *Don't Bother Me Mom, I'm Learning!: How Computer and Video Games Are Preparing Your Kids for 21st-Century Success and How You Can Help!* (St. Paul, MN: Paragon House, 2006), pp. 27–31.

44. D. Michael and S. Chen, *Serious Games: Games That Educate, Train, and Inform* (Boston: Thomson, 2006).

45. T. Susi, M. Johannesson, and P. Backlund, *Serious Games: An Overview* (technical report HS-IKI-TR-07-001, School of Humanities and Informatics University of Skövde, Sweden, 2007), p. 11, retrieved from http://his.diva-portal.org/smash/get/diva2:2416/FULLTEXT01.

46. Ibid., p. 14.

47. See http://www.gamesthatwork.com.

48. J. Kirriemuir and A. McFarlane, "Literature Review in Games and Learning," *Futurelab Report* 8 (2004): 19, retrieved from www.coulthard.com/library/Files/kirriemuir-futurelabs_2004_gamesreview.pdf.

49. Klopfer and S. Osterweil, "Boom and Bust and Boom," pp. 290–96.

50. V. Shute and J. Psotka, "Intelligent Tutoring Systems: Past, Present, and Future," in *Handbook of Research on Educational Communications and Technology*, ed. D. Jonassen (New York: Macmillan Library Reference, 1996), pp. 572–74.

51. V. Shute, "Regarding the *I* in ITS: Student Modeling," *Proceedings of ED-MEDIA 94: World Conference on Educational Multimedia and Hypermedia, Vancouver* (1994), p. 50.

52. H. Newquist, *The Brain Makers: Genius, Ego, and Greed and the Quest for Machines That Think* (Indianapolis, IN: Sams Publishing, 1994), pp. 12–17.

53. Papert, *Mindstorms*, p. 157.

54. B. Bloom, "The 2-sigma Problem: The Search for Methods of Group Instruction as Effective as One-to-One Tutoring," *Educational Researcher* 13, no. 6 (1984): 4–16.

55. P. Brusilovsky and C. Peylo, "Adaptive and Intelligent Web-Based Educational Systems," in *International Journal of Artificial Intelligence in Education* 13, nos. 2–4 (2003): 159–72.

56. Shute and Psotka, "Intelligent Tutoring Systems," pp. 574–76.

57. V. Shute, "SMART: Student Modeling Approach for Responsive Tutoring," *User Modeling and User-Adapted Instruction* 5 (1995): 5–10.

58. D. Bobrow, "Dimensions of Representation," In *Representation and Understanding*, ed. D. Bobrow and A. Collins (New York: Academic Press, 1979), pp. 1–34.

59. R. Burton and J. Brown, "An Investigation of Computer Coaching for Informal Learning Activities," in *Intelligent Tutoring Systems*, ed. D. Sleeman and J. Brown (London: Academic Press, 1982), pp. 79–98.

60. J. Anderson, *The Architecture of Cognition* (Cambridge, MA: Harvard University Press, 1983), pp. 1–44.

61. J. Anderson, A. Corbett, K. Koedinger, and R. Pelletier, "Cognitive Tutors: Lessons Learned," *Journal of Learning Sciences* 4 (1995): 167–207.

62. Valerie Shute, personal communication, Nov. 17, 2004.

63. Shute, "SMART," p. 5.

64. B. Du Boulay, "Can We Learn from ITSs?" (invited talk at the 5th International Conference on Intelligent Tutoring Systems, Montreal, 2000).

65. Shute, "SMART," pp. 21–23.

66. E. El-Sheikh, "An Architecture for the Generation of Intelligent Tutoring Systems from Reusable Components and Knowledge-Based Systems" (PhD diss., Michigan State University, 2002).

67. K. Koedinger, J. Anderson, W. Hadley, and M. Mark, "Intelligent Tutoring Goes to School in the Big City," *International Journal of Artificial Intelligence in Education* 8 (1997): 30–43.

68. L. Jerinic and V. Devedžic, "A Friendly Intelligent Tutoring Environment," *SIGCHI Bulletin* 32, no. 1 (2000): 83–94.

69. Peter Brusilovsky, personal communication, Aug. 22, 2013.

Chapter 5. From the Cloud

1. Retrieved from http://en.wikiquote.org/wiki/Yogi_Berra.

2. T. Foster, "Instruction by Correspondence," *American Machinist* 29 (1906): 584.

3. T. Kidd, *Online Education and Adult Learning: New Frontiers for Teaching Practices* (Hershey PA: Information Science Reference, 2010), pp. 35–36.

4. Ibid., p. 40.

5. J. Hechinger, "For-Profit College Slump Converging with Student Life-Debtors," *Bloomberg Business News*, Dec. 28, 2010.

6. C. Beha, "Leveling the Field: What I Learned from For-Profit Education," *Harper's*, Dec. 2011, pp. 52–57.

7. V. Connell, "False Hopes Meet False Claims: Consumer Perils in For-Profit Education and Recommendations for Legal Remedies" (2012), retrieved from http://ssrn.com/abstract=1991123.

8. The University of Phoenix is owned by the public Apollo Group; see www.nasdaq.com/symbol/apol.

9. Beha, "Leveling the Field," p. 54.

10. L. Vincent, *John Heyl Vincent: A Biographical Sketch* (New York: Macmillan, 1925), pp. 130–31.

11. Retrieved from www.open.ac.uk/about/main/the-ou-explained/facts-and-figures.

12. Retrieved from www.k12.com/what-is-k12/how-k12-education-work.

13. G. Stern, "Company Training Programs: What Are They Really Worth?" *CNN Money*, May 27, 2011, retrieved from http://management.fortune.cnn.com/2011/05/27/company-training-programs-what-are-they-really-worth.

14. R. Ubell, "The Road Not Taken: The Divergence of Corporate and Academic Web Instruction," *Journal of Asynchronous Learning Networks* 14, no. 2 (2010): 3.

15. W. Watson, "An Argument for Clarity: What Are Learning Management Systems, What Are They Not, and What Should They Become?" *TechTrends* 51, no. 2 (2007): 30.

16. H. Coates, R. James, and G. Baldwin, "A Critical Examination of the Effects of Learning Management Systems on University Teaching and Learning," *Tertiary Education and Management* 11, no. 1 (2005): 20–21.

17. S. Malikowski, M. Thompson, and J. Theis, "A Model for Research into Course Management Systems: Bridge Technology and Learning Theory," *Journal of Educational Computing Research* 36, no. 2 (2007): 149–73.

18. J. Mott, "Envisioning the Post-LMS Era: The Open Learning Network," *Educause Review*, Mar. 3, 2010, retrieved from www.educause.edu/ero/article/envisioning-post -lms-era-open-learning-network.

19. Coates, James, and Baldwin, "Critical Examination," pp. 23–24.

20. Mott, "Envisioning the Post-LMS Era."

21. Coates, James, and Baldwin, "Critical Examination," p. 27.

22. G. Alexander, *Academic Films for the Classroom: A History* (Jefferson, NC: McFarland, 2010), p. 27.

23. See www.ed.gov/policy/gen/guid/fpco/ferpa/index.html.

24. For more information on LTI, see www.imsglobal.org/toolsinteroperability2.cfm.

25. Khan Academy, "Press Fact Sheet" (Aug. 2013), retrieved from www.khanacademy .org.

26. S. Khan, *The One World Schoolhouse: Education Reimagined* (New York: Twelve, 2012), p. 15.

27. Ibid., pp. 186–88.

28. C. Thompson, "The New Way to Be a Fifth Grader," *Wired* 19, no. 8 (Aug. 11, 2011): 128.

29. Khan, *One World Schoolhouse*, pp. 16–22.

30. Ibid., p. 23.

31. Ibid., p. 25.

32. Thompson, "New Way to Be a Fifth Grader," p. 126.

33. Khan, *One World Schoolhouse*, 34–35.

34. M. Noer, "Reeducating Education," *Forbes* 190, no. 9 (Nov. 19, 2012), p. 98.

35. Khan Academy, "Press Fact Sheet."

36. Peter Brusilovsky, personal communication, Aug. 22, 2013.

37. M. Prensky, "Khan Academy," *Educational Technology*, July–Aug. 2011.

38. B. Victor, "Learnable Programming" (2013), retrieved from http://worrydream .com/LearnableProgramming.

39. "Bret Victor: Inventing on Principle" (video from CUSEC 2012), retrieved from http://vimeo.com/36579366.

40. Ibid.

41. A. McAuley, B. Stewart, G. Siemens, and D. Cormier, "The MOOC Model for Digital Practice," *SSHRC Knowledge Synthesis Grant on the Digital Economy* (2010), pp. 21–22, retrieved from http://davecormier.com/edblog/wp-content/uploads/MOOC_ Final.pdf.

42. G. Siemens, "What Is Connectivism?" in *Connectivism and Connective Knowledge MOOC* (Sept. 8, 2008), retrieved from http://elearnspace.org/media/WhatIsConnectivism /player.html.

43. McAuley et al., "MOOC Model," pp. 22–23.

44. Dave Cormier, personal communication, Sept. 12, 2013.

45. S. Hargadon, "A True History of the MOOC" (webinar, Sept. 26, 2012), retrieved from www.stevehargadon.com/2012/09/tonight-true-history-of-mooc.html.

46. D. Cormier, "The CCK08 MOOC-Connectivism course, 1/4 way" (blog post, Oct. 2, 2008), retrieved from http://davecormier.com/edblog/2008/10/02/the-cck08-mooc-connectivism-course-14-way.

47. McAuley et al., "MOOC Model," p. 23.

48. Hargadon, "True History"; for the quote from character Ian Malcolm, see M. Crichton, *Jurassic Park* (New York: Ballantine, 2012), p. 179.

49. S. Leckart, "The Stanford Education Experiment Could Change Higher Learning Forever," *Wired* 20, no. 4 (2012): 68.

50. C. Rodriguez, "MOOCs and the AI-Stanford Like Courses: Two Successful and Distinct Course Formats for Massive Open Online Courses," *European Journal of Open, Distance and E-learning* 3 (2012), pp. 7–8, retrieved from www.eurodl.org/materials/contrib/2012/Rodriguez.pdf.

51. T. Vanderbilt, "How Artificial Intelligence Can Change Education," *Smithsonian*, Dec. 2012, retrieved from www.smithsonianmag.com/people-places/How-Artificial-Intelligence-Can-Change-Higher-Education-180015811.html.

52. Ibid.

53. See "Sebastian Thrun: Google's Driverless Car" (March 2011), retrieved from www.ted.com/talks/sebastian_thrun_google_s_driverless_car.html, and "Let's Use Video to Reinvent Education: Salman Khan on TED.com" (Mar. 9, 2011), retrieved from http://blog.ted.com/2011/03/09/lets-use-video-to-reinvent-education-salman-khan-on-ted-com/.

54. Leckart, "Stanford Education Experiment," p. 68.

55. A. Stepan, "Massive Open Online Courses (MOOC) Disruptive Impact on Higher Education" (MBA thesis, Simon Fraser University, 2013), p. 87.

56. Leckart, "Stanford Education Experiment," p. 68.

57. T. Friedman, "Come the Revolution," *New York Times*, May 15, 2012, retrieved from www.nytimes.com/2012/05/16/opinion/friedman-come-the-revolution.html.

58. J. Wiener, "Inside the Coursera Hype Machine," *The Nation*, Sept. 23, 2013, retrieved from www.thenation.com/article/176036/inside-coursera-hype-machine.

59. N. Carr, "The Crisis in Higher Education," *Technology Review* 115, no. 6 (2012): 35.

60. D. Koller, "This Week in Startups" (video, Aug. 27, 2013), retrieved from www.youtube.com/watch?v=AzcuofM1QkI.

61. S. Mitra, "I Want to Teach Engineering to a Billion: Anant Agarwal, President of EdX" (blog post, Feb. 14, 2013), retrieved from www.sramanamitra.com/2013/02/14/i-want-to-teach-engineering-to-a-billion-anant-agarwal-president-of-edx-part-1.

62. P. Nanda, "Learn Anytime, Anywhere and Largely for Free: Anant Agarwal," *Livemint/Wall Street Journal*, Aug. 3, 2013, retrieved from www.livemint.com/Politics/TFqJqM6l4K39Q2gq8JNg5O/Learn-anytime-anywhere-and-largely-for-free-Anant-Agarwal.html.

63. P. Mitro, K. Affidi, G. Sussman, C. Terman, J. White, L. Fischer, and A. Agarwal, "Teaching Electronic Circuits Online: Lessons for MITx's 6.002 on edX," *IEEE Circuits and Systems ISCAS* (2013), pp. 2763–66.

64. T. Lewin, "One Course, 150,000 Students," *New York Times*, July 22, 2012, retrieved from www.nytimes.com/2012/07/20/education/edlife/anant-agarwal-discusses-free-online-courses-offered-by-a-harvard-mit-partnership.html.

65. "Harvard and MIT Announce edX," (MIT press release, 2012), retrieved from http://web.mit.edu/press/2012/mit-harvard-edx-announcement.html.

66. See www.edx.org/schools.

67. Nanda, "Learn Anytime."

68. R. Kunze, *Nothing Ventured: The Perils and Payoffs of the Great American Venture Capital Game* (New York: HarperCollins, 1991).

69. P. Carlson and F. Berry, "Calibrated Peer Review and Assessing Learning Outcomes" (presented at the 33rd ASEE/IEEE Frontiers in Education Conference, 2003), pp. F3E 2–F3E 3.

70. K. Kukich, "Beyond Automated Essay Scoring," *IEEE Intelligent Systems* 15, no. 5 (2000): 22–27.

71. B. Ferster, T. Hammond, R. Alexander, and H. Lyman, "Automated Formative Assessment as a Tool to Scaffold Student Documentary Writing," *Journal of Interactive Learning Research* 23, no. 1 (2012): 81–99.

72. J. Wang and M. Brown, "Automated Essay Scoring versus Human Scoring: A Comparative Study," *Journal of Technology, Learning, and Assessment* 6, no. 2 (2007): 20–22.

73. J. Markoff, "Essay-Grading Software Offers Professors a Break," *New York Times*, Apr. 4, 2013, retrieved from www.nytimes.com/2013/04/05/science/new-test-for-computers -grading-essays-at-college-level.html. For Professionals against Machine Scoring of Student Essays in High-Stakes Assessment, see http://humanreaders.org.

74. J. Mangalindan, "Amazon's Recommendation Secret," *Fortune*, July 30, 2012, retrieved from http://tech.fortune.cnn.com/2012/07/30/amazon-5.

75. P. Spring, P. Leeflang, and T. Wansbeek, "The Combination Strategy to Optimal Target Selection and Offer Segmentation in Direct Mail," *Journal of Market-Focused Management* 4, no. 3 (1999): 87–203.

76. B. Christian, "The A/B Test: Inside the Technology That's Changing the Rules of Business," *Wired* 20, no. 5 (2012): 176.

77. Daphne Koller, personal communication, Feb. 20, 2013.

78. Carr, "Crisis in Higher Education," p. 39.

79. W. Bowen, "The 'Cost Disease' in Higher Education: Is Technology the Answer?" (Tanner Lectures on Human Values, Stanford University, Oct. 11, 2012).

80. C. Shirky, "MOOCs and Economic Reality," *Chronicle of Higher Education* 59, no. 42 (2013): 3.

Chapter 6. Making Sense of Teaching Machines

1. B. Bloom, "The 2-sigma Problem: The Search for Methods of Group Instruction as Effective as One-to-One Tutoring," *Educational Researcher* 13, no. 6 (1984): 4–16.

2. E. Rogers, *Diffusion of Innovations*, 4th ed. (New York: Free Press, 1995), pp. 261–68.

3. E. Rushton, *Programmed Learning: The Roanoke Experiment* (Chicago: Encyclopedia Britannica Press, 1965), p. 37.

4. J. Kett, *Merit: The History of a Founding Ideal from the American Revolution to the 21st Century* (Ithaca, NY: Cornell University Press, 2013), p. 112.

5. Joe Garofalo, personal communication, Oct. 7, 2013.

6. W. Harms and I. DePencier, *100 Years of Learning at the University of Chicago Laboratory School* (Chicago: University of Chicago Laboratory Schools, 1996), chap. 3, retrieved from www.ucls.uchicago.edu/about-lab/history.

7. Ibid.

8. J. Bransford, A. Brown, and R. Cocking, eds., *How People Learn: Brain, Mind, Experience, and School* (Washington, DC: National Academy Press, 1999), p. 78.

9. B. F. Skinner, *A Matter of Consequences* (New York: Knopf, 1983), p. 64.

10. Bloom, "2-sigma Problem."

11. Roger, *Diffusion of Innovations*, pp. 242–51.

12. D. Norman, *The Design of Everyday Things* (New York: Basic Books, 1988), pp. 81–131.

13. B. Ferster, "Toward a Predictive Model of the Diffusion of Technology into the K–12 Classroom" (PhD diss., University of Virginia, 2006), pp. 111–12.

14. Salomon Berner, personal communication, Aug. 1987.

15. T. Foster, "Instruction by Correspondence," *American Machinist* 29 (1906): 587.

16. J. Eayrs, *Diplomacy and Its Discontents* (Toronto: University of Toronto Press, 1971), p. 121.

17. D. Norman, *Things That Make Us Smart: Defending Human Attributes in the Age of the Machine* (Reading, MA: Addison-Wesley, 1993), p. 253.

18. B. Skinner, "Teaching Machines," *Science* 243, no. 4898 (1989): 1535.

Index